THE POWER WITHIN

THE POWER WITHIN

Clara Endicott Sears

Forewords by Ellen Ratner
and Cholene Espinoza

Changing Lives Press
50 Public Square #1600
Cleveland, OH 44113
www.changinglivespress.com

Library of Congress Cataloging-in-Publication Data is available through the Library of Congress.

ISBN-10: 0-9837515-8-7
ISBN-13: 978-0-9837515-8-8

Cover & interior design: Gary A. Rosenberg

Printed in the United States of America

10 9 8 7 6 5 4 3 2 1

This little volume must
radiate serenity and happiness
in order to fulfill its mission.

The writings of the following authors are quoted in *The Power Within:*

Annie Payson Call

Aaron Martin Crane

Horatio W. Dresser

Ralph Waldo Emerson

Christian D. Larson

Orison Swett Marden

Annie Rix Militz

Prentice Mulford

Charles B. Newcomb

Katherine H. Newcomb

Elizabeth Towne

Henry Wood

Lilian Whiting

FOREWORD by Ellen Ratner

TWENTY YEARS AGO, when I first started writing *Self Empowerment: Nine Things the 19th Century Can Teach Us About Living in the 21st,* a friend invited me to look at a carton of books in his attic. I found this little volume and put it away. Then, as Anne Gehman and I were finishing *Self Empowerment,* I took it out and gave it to Cholene Espinoza, who was finishing her first year of medical school at St. Georges University in Grenada. I thought the wisdom in *The Power Within* would help her in her studies. She loved it and we decided to re-publish the book.

Clara Endicott Sears was born to a wealthy New England family and started Fruitlands

Museum in Harvard, Massachusetts. In the mid-1970's, I lived up the road from Fruitlands, which houses both an old Shaker House and the Fruitlands Farm House of Bronson Alcott (Lousia May Alcott's father). Ms. Sears wrote many books, and in 1911 she decided to compile her favorite quotes from the New Thought and Transcendental authors. She published only enough books for her and her friends and years later published it for others.

Ms. Sears wrote in her foreword: "The thoughts this little book contains cannot fail to give poise to those who have lost their bearings; a reasonable and well-founded joy to those who have become disheartened, and a law of living which makes even the rough places along the path seem worthwhile. They have done this for me, they will do it for you. I have never known them to fail."

We debated changing the pronouns from "him" to "her" and "one" but decided to leave it in its original form.

We hope that this book will give you as much inspiration as it has given to us.

Ellen Ratner
Washington, D.C.
December 2011

FOREWORD by Cholene Espinoza

THE DAILY THOUGHTS EXPRESSED in this little book were written over a hundred years ago. Yet they breathed new life into me at a time when I was giving my "power" away. Stressed with trials of medical school at the age of forty-six, missing the life of adventure I once knew as a pilot, uncertain of my future in this new field, and generally disoriented, one night I opened *The Power Within.* I thought it would help me sleep—to make the props in my mind stop spinning after a day of studying.

The passage I randomly opened to instantly liberated me from the anxiety, self-doubt, disorientation, and loneliness that were always simmering beneath my "fake it 'til you make it" exterior. I found reassurance, confidence, calm, a return to centeredness, and conviction of purpose. I claimed for the first time, my Power Within and I embraced the love and momentum of a spirit that transcends the confines of the human mind. It is my hope that you will as well.

Tailwinds and blessings,
Cholene Espinoza

FOREWORD by Clara Endicott Sears

At one time I had the contents of this little volume privately printed in a convenient form so that I might carry it about with me for perusal at odd moments throughout the day. I had a few to give to friends who I knew were in sympathy with the thoughts it contains. These friends loaned their copies to others, with the result that an ever-growing demand for them has made it almost a necessity to have the collection published in due form, so that those who desire them can procure them.

The thoughts this little book contains cannot fail to give poise to those who have lost their bearings; —a reasonable and well-founded joy to those who have become disheartened, and a law of living which makes even the rough places along the path seem worth while.

They have done this for me.

They will do it for you.

I have never known them to fail.

—*Clara Endicott Sears*

THE POWER WITHIN

January 1

The life of every day would be a pleasure, if we would permit ourselves to enjoy the work in hand. Disease and misfortune result from habits of mind. We cannot have a sickly body or environment without a sickly thought behind it. Our mental attitude *today* determines our success *tomorrow.*

—Newcomb.

January 2

Great men are they who see that spiritual force is stronger than material force;— that thoughts rule the world.

—Emerson.

After any object or purpose is clearly held in thought, its precipitation, in tangible and visible form, is merely a question of time. Columbus saw in vision a path through trackless waters around the world. The vision always precedes, and itself determines the realization.

—Whiting.

January 3

It is as important to relax our minds as it is to concentrate them. Relaxation and concentration are opposite poles of the same mental currents. It is desirable that we understand and alternate these conditions wisely, else we shall be always either tense or scattered. Our weariness comes from ignorance of our powers. Usually it results from mental friction of some sort, rather than excessive activity.

—Newcomb.

January 4

The great problem of human life is one of adjustment to environment. When this has been achieved, the mastery of conditions follows. Suffering comes from mental resentment. The first impulse arising from discomfort leads one to resent and resist. As we grow wiser we learn that antagonism is itself a cause of pain. No problem can come into any life which is not for that life to solve.

—Newcomb.

January 5

Man's spirit is buoyant, and nothing can resist our upward progress except our own determination to resist it. All the powers of nature but typify the power of man. No day can come or go without enriching us to the full extent to which we have developed our capacity to receive. To the spirit that has come to realize its power, there is no such thing as fear.

–Newcomb.

January 6

There is not a creature in God's universe without the instinct for perfection. No one is left without guidance. No one can sink into a pit of darkness so deep that the divine spark cannot be kindled. This is the lesson of all sorrow, of all suffering, of all persecution for the sake of truth. Immanent in our very hardships is the perfecting power of God. All our trials and tribulations are blessings in disguise. Why need we suffer? because suffering teaches what naught else can teach;—because we do not really know until we have personally struggled and sorrowed – and conquered.

—Dresser.

January 7

So long as the nature of your personal action is no better than the environment in which you live, you will continue in that environment, but the moment you begin to improve the quality, the power, and the efficiency of your personal action, you will positively have the opportunity to enter better environments.

—C. D. Larson.

January 8

A man may as truly dwell in the Kingdom of Heaven while still in the flesh, as one who has left the flesh life forever. For there is no future state of perfection into which the good suddenly enter at death. The tomorrow of death is the logical sequence of today in the flesh. The only standard by which a man is judged is character,—spiritual worth,—spiritual consciousness. If a man awakens today to the knowledge of his life with God, he comes into possession of knowledge which death cannot take away.

—Dresser.

January 9

If a man is born into the future life in ignorance, he must patiently work his way to heavenly knowledge. The presence or absence of spiritual consciousness is thus the vital fact. No occupation is so burdensome that it cannot be made an opportunity for the growth of character. No tyrant is so cruel that the oppressed may not display sweetness, and love, and forgiveness. No condition is unfavorable for the display of love. The ideal day never comes. Today is ideal for him who makes it so.

—Dresser.

January 10

A truly concentrated life promptly rejects every thought of past or future that would disturb its confidence in the present hour. It accepts nothing that will not feed its power. Success results from confident demand upon the higher self. When we fail, it is because our purposes are easily broken off.

–Newcomb.

January 11

As we become aroused to the higher vibrations of spirit, we become indifferent to the lower vibrations of matter, knowing we can control them. Health and prosperity result from our awaking to consciousness of spiritual power. Inflammation, fever and congestion are the natural results of interrupted circulation in thought life. Our fears are always premature and lead us to confusion.

—Newcomb.

January 12

Non-resistance to evil should never be non-activity. The same energy which would spend itself as hate, must be turned to the gentler but far more effective channel of love. For love is a mighty power, able to master evil, and only by being true to its guidance may we ever hope to win the day for righteousness.

A man may compromise with his conscience, if he will, but he will not find the Kingdom. He may simulate righteousness, but he will have a corresponding reward. Man alone is at fault. The wrong springs from within. All reform must accordingly begin within. The law is so plain that in the end even the fool cannot err therein.

—Dresser.

January 13

We are *always* responsible for our mental condition. Nothing but our personal choice demands that we shall respond to false vibrations. We have the power to strike and hold any keynote at will. We need not come into another's discord,–or be distressed that it exists. We cannot help another beyond our power to bestow, and his ability to receive.

–Newcomb.

January 14

God is to be judged not by the passing event, which may inadequately reveal Him, but by what He is making of and through the universe during all ages. The soul cannot be truly understood by this or that deed alone, which may even misrepresent the true man, but by its life as a whole when seen from the point of view of motive and individuality. The outward expression must ever be imperfect, since the soul unceasingly presses forward.

–H. Dresser.

January 15

What must I do, is all that concerns me,—not what people think. It is easy in the world to live after the world's opinion; it is easy in solitude to live after our own;—but the great man is he who in the midst of the crowd keeps with perfect sweetness the independence of solitude.

—Emerson.

January 16

Believe in your ideals, even when you are surrounded with everything but that which is ideal, and things will positively take a turn. Do not come down, though everything in your world seems to be down. Stand by your lofty position, and the highest powers in your being will stand by you. Things will soon come up, adversity will disappear, the sunshine of good fortune will return, and a larger, richer, happier world will open its doors to you.

–C. D. Larson.

January 17

Every day we are developing new conditions of ultimate success. Not only that, but every day is in itself successful, even though no progress is apparent. Our simple effort has at least developed wind and muscle, making us stronger than yesterday, and better equipped for the work at which we aim. If we indulge ourselves in tragic mood and moments of despondency and doubt, we only increase and complicate our tasks. We dull the axe with which we hew, and thus compel ourselves to put forth more strength.

–Newcomb.

January 18

It is absolutely necessary to the highest success that we rid ourselves of the fever of impatience, and throw off the disease of indecision and uncertainty. All the world suffers from a mental "grippe" for want of real belief in the absolute good. Persistent confidence is the first requisite in any undertaking, if we wish to arrive at positive results. Such confidence makes delays and disappointment quite unnecessary, if it is prepared to stand them as tests of our strength.

–Newcomb.

January 19

An ideal is a responsibility,—it is the working model that God has set before the individual,—the pattern after which and by which he shall shape his life. If he accept and follow it with fidelity and energy,—with that energy horn of absolute faith in the divine leading,—he will find himself miraculously led,—he will find that the obstacle which appears so insurmountable in perspective, vanishes as he comes near,—that a way is made,—a path appears.

—Whiting.

January 20

As long as you radiate doubt and discouragement, you will be a failure. If you want to get away from poverty, you must keep your mind in a productive, creative condition. In order to do this you must think confident, cheerful creative thoughts. The model must precede the statue. You must see a new world before you can live in it.

–O. S. Marden.

January 21

Spiritual energy is an infinite force; –the more it is drawn upon, the larger is the supply, and it is given to man to use, and to use *here* and *now.* It is his birthright. Spirituality in life lies in recognizing and using this exhaustless force to create the conditions in which one may be the most useful to others, and in which he shall find the greatest happiness and harmony for himself.

–Whiting.

January 22

The first lesson of power is to learn that all possibilities centre in the individual will. We are so apt to look upon ourselves as captives, until there comes a day when a new light shines into our soul,—our fetters are broken, and we go free. There is never a moment in life when any of us can really justify discouragement.

—Newcomb.

January 23

The *cause* of whatever comes to you in life is within you. There is where it is created. The thing you long for and work for comes to you because your thought has created it,—because there is something within you that attracts it. It comes because there is an affinity within you for it. Your own comes to you,—is always seeking you.

—O. S. Marden.

January 24

It is not circumstances that make us, but *we make circumstances.* Complaint, and indecision, and depression, and doubt, plant the seeds of failure, while confidence, and faith, and optimism plant the seeds of success. Both will flower and bring forth of their own kind.

—K. H. Newcomb.

January 25

He who looks with steadfastness to his highest ideal, will with the utmost certainty realize it. And, as he approaches its realization, he will find still higher ideals forming in him. The free and constant inspiration of the Almighty, giveth him higher and yet higher understanding.

–E. Towne.

January 26

Until we are free from all anxiety regarding any matter, we are not master of it. Can you not see that you must develop? You must have openness of mind–receptivity. Some people are living in pint pots with the covers down. Where are you living?

–K. H. Newcomb.

January 27

The essence of prayer is soul hunger,—a yearning after oneness with the eternal. It is the breath of the spiritual nature, the native air of the soul. It is a vital law in man's nature that this highest faculty shall be exercised.

We do not suffer except as we abide in darkness. We are not forced to violent effort to dispel this darkness. We need only *let in* the light.

—Wood.

January 28

The ebb and flow of will is like the movements of the tides. The sense of weakness and of power alternates in every life, until the negative condition is outgrown through mastery. We are warranted in boldly claiming that we have no limitations except those we have placed on ourselves. The soul cannot grow in the atmosphere of fear.

—Newcomb.

January 29

We must eliminate *every particle* of the poison of fear from our minds, before we can arrive at the perfect peace which cometh through understanding. Fear is only indolence of will. We need only arouse ourselves to spiritual consciousness and we find that we live amid incalculable forces,—which we ourselves control when the divine part of us is awakened.

—Newcomb.

January 30

Live in the upper story of mind and give soul to all your thought; you will thereby form ideas with real quality and worth. No person can afford to take a commonplace view of anything, nor to indulge in cheap thinking at any time; –to do so is to place inferior seeds in the garden of the mind. What enters the subconscious of any mind and will, to a degree affects the nature, the character, the quality, the thoughts, and the actions of that mind. Right thinking deeply felt will bring health, harmony, peace, power, ability and character. What we mentally feel we invariably impress upon the subconscious.

–C. D. Larson.

January 31

Prove that you can keep your inner joy in the midst of sorrow, and hold your place in the midst of irritations and threatening depression, and you know that from thenceforth no man can take your joy or your peace from you. You have the fountain in your soul.

—A. R. Militz.

We should think of joy as coming from Spirit, and therefore as unaffected or unchanged by things external to us. If we think that external things have power to make us joyful, by the same reasoning we think of them as having power to destroy our joy. If we know the Truth and abide in the constant and eternal joy of Spirit, we shall not be sad at times and joyful at others. Our joy is established in Spirit.

—Unity Daily Word.

February 1

We cannot play the chords of "success" upon an instrument relaxed by disappointment and discouragement, nor with the harp-strings held at nervous tension by anxiety and fear. Only a masterful confidence in the Universal Life and in ourselves as its expression, can strike the notes of power, and produce the clear, full tones in which true purpose finds complete accomplishment.

–Newcomb.

February 2

When some one is angry with you, and fault is found with you, instead of beginning to defend yourself and to answer back in the same spirit, turn your attention inward, and down every resentful thought with these words: "None of these things move me."–[St. Paul.] Always speak these words silently, not aloud, else you antagonize the other. Practice repeating these words at the approach of every annoying thought, even the most trivial events of your life, for it is by control over one's self in the little things of life that one has self-possession when the great things are facing him.

–A. R. Militz.

February 3

It is a source of happiness if we habitually look for good wherever we go, and in this way show our superiority to all that is belittling and mean. We shall soon find no time for complaint and discouragement if we undertake to live in this attitude of mind. Our eyes will open to new beauties in nature and in human life. We shall gradually learn to see life through the artist's eyes,—to look for its poetry, its harmony, its divine meaning.

—Dresser.

February 4

We may pass through almost any experience if we realize that the power residing within is equal to the occasion. When we cease to look upon any experience as "too hard," we have made a decided step in wise adjustment to life. Life itself becomes easier and happier when we make this grand discovery, that within each human soul there is a sufficient resource for every need along the line of the individual career. We can conquer anything through the divine leading.

—Dresser.

February 5

True principle is always robust. It is spiritual knowledge, and has in it no element of indecision or distrust. It stands unmoved by temporary appearances, and has unwavering confidence in everlasting good for every life. It admits no doubt or failure possible, but holds to the assurance that the higher self of every one will eventually claim its right to govern.

–Newcomb.

February 6

The facts of time are not distressing to one who lives in the larger fact of the eternal. It is not persuasion or environment that reforms a life, but the awakening of its own innate energies. These alone have power to renew the purpose, vitalize the will, and guide the destinies that we are helpless to control for one another.

—Newcomb.

February 7

Life contains a full provision for us all. There is no lack to any human being who is ready to obey the laws of harmony. Confidence is the first lesson in the spiritual primer, and full realization is the last. Indecision is a fatal disease wherever it appears. It withers and kills through inactivity and stagnation. No battle was ever won under the banner of "I can't."

–Newcomb.

February 8

The only real power is that which radiates from character. All our fancied limitations lie in the artificial conditions we create. They do not belong to the real man as his environment. We are slow to accept the truth of our infinity. Sooner or later we arrive at its recognition.

–Newcomb.

February 9

Truth awaits our pleasure. Its acceptance is a matter of choice to every individual. We can never exaggerate the intelligence or power of the spirit. Every demonstration comes to us at the moment we are prepared to welcome it. We must needs break down the walls of doubt and indecision we have built about us before we can obtain the evidence we seek,–as we must open our eyes before we can see the sun.

–Newcomb.

February 10

Success is quite impossible to him who throws his energies into the forging of thought fetters, and hears only the voice of his lesser self. The value of experience is greater than we can understand while under the stress that it involves. We torture and wound ourselves in every hour of sojourning in the land of indecision. When we once have passed the barriers our doubts have raised, we find an open way to power.

–Newcomb.

February 11

True thought will lead to action, but the power is in the thought more than in the action. When we cultivate thoughts of strength for others, we ourselves grow strong. Habitual thoughts of peace bring us tranquillity. The thoughts of opulence will naturally result in wealth if rightly held. If all of Wisdom's ways "are ways of pleasantness and all her paths are peace," there is nothing more unrighteous than disease and poverty.

–Newcomb.

February 12

Through all the weaving of mortal and immortal life runs the golden thread of spiritual consciousness. As we gradually awaken, we perceive that life itself is a perpetual miracle. A selfish life dulls all our senses, and makes us both deaf and blind to our highest good. Our lives should not be governed by the opinions of others. The only matter of importance is that we should *deserve* to think well of ourselves.

—Newcomb.

February 13

Nature's resources are not limited by our perceptions. It cannot be suppressed when once awakened. Its energies cannot long be confined after the awakening. Man may choose the channels through which this tireless energy shall have its largest expression in his personal life. According to his choice will he manifest power. The highest expression makes the strongest demand upon the Infinite Source, and results in the largest growth.

–Newcomb.

February 14

Suppression is not dominion. We must *root out* and exterminate the wrong beliefs–the mental weeds. We must plough and harrow the ground, and plant an entirely new crop of goodly thoughts. Only in this way can we become proprietors of our fields,–the lords of our domains. Freedom and disease and poverty can never exist together. The one inevitably destroys the other. We may choose between them, but can never hold them both.

–Newcomb.

February 15

Heaviness of spirit is never imposed upon us without our consent. Life is never niggardly of its gladness, if only we will be receptive to it. Wherever we find a special difficulty of environment or weakness of character, we also find, if we look closely, a special faculty for grappling with it. With every need there is some resource with which it can be met. For all supply in nature's wonderful expression has been developed in response to special demand.

–Newcomb.

February 16

The soul is like a firefly or glowworm. It radiates an inner light which illumines its own way. It possesses the magnetic power by which it can draw to itself the people and things it finds desirable. Our spiritual radiations meet and mingle with those of other lives that are attuned to ours. Distance cannot separate us. We are guided to places and occupations and surroundings where we can best work out our destiny.

—Newcomb.

February 17

The mysterious forces emanating from ourselves govern our environment at every moment. In our journeyings they guide our choice of routes and plans of travel. In library or bookstore these invisible rays search out and bring to our attention that which we find helpful, no matter how remotely it may be hidden and shelved. In what appears to be accidental ways, peculiar paragraphs, and pages that we need are brought before our eyes.

—Newcomb.

February 18

There is no search-light of man's invention which is anything more than a poor suggestion of the spiritual intelligence enlightening every human being. No magnet equals it in its attracting power. The universe is the field of its radiant energy. Its currents are as irresistible as the law of gravitation. It is the expression of the same infinite wisdom which has provided for the sparrow and the lily.

–Newcomb.

February 19

Life is strong and true in its expression only when *purpose* and *action* are united and allied with *will*. Never for one instant should we give lodgment to an untrue thought. It opens the door to serious results, and puts our instrument out of tune. Impatience is explosive. We can no more predict the result of setting it free than we can tell the spot where lightning will strike when it has torn its way through the cloud, and descended earthward.

–Newcomb.

February 20

When we are confident of the strength of our position, our tones are steady, our speech is calm, and the entire expression of voice and action is in harmony with our highest thought. Nature's chromatic scale has many octaves. The Universal Energy finds utterance in weeds as well as flowers, fruits, and forests. The same creative forces are at work in all.

–Newcomb.

February 21

The divine principle which is within every human being will *sometime* manifest itself, for all are made in the image and likeness of supreme good. We cannot believe in God and refuse to believe in man. Much of our distress at sin and suffering results from want of understanding of the principles that govern life. It is our fickleness and cowardice that oftenest defeat our aims. The man who dares and perseveres is the man who wins.

–Newcomb.

February 22

If we are not satisfied with what our lives express in their environment and bodily conditions, we must alter our point of view, and destroy our fears. Freedom is to be had only on these terms. Back of all unrest is wrong thinking, and fear, gnawing like a worm at the root of happiness. The imperfect results that we show in our activities are largely due to indecision and uncertainty of purpose.

–Newcomb.

February 23

Nature insists upon perfection, and all defective types carry the seeds of their own destruction. All healthy life perpetuates itself with an increasing power and momentum. We believe that the law that governs the universe governs every single planet of its system, and every detail of the animal, vegetable and mineral kingdoms—and we include the individual life of man in the law. We recognize a Universal Power and with it we identify the divine in man.

—Newcomb.

February 24

Every imperfect and false note that has been struck in the attempt of the race to master the harmonies of life has left its vibrations in earth's atmosphere. Science asserts that all vibrations are eternal, whether of light or sound. Thus every act of a human being must be stamped into his surroundings, but the vibrations of love and service and unselfishness are stronger than all others, and reach the farthest.

–Newcomb.

February 25

Until one has developed his individuality, he is constantly subject to the discordant currents which emanate from the mental atmosphere of those about us. As his own thought becomes more definite in its aims, and positive in character, he ceases to suffer from the thoughts of others. Nothing can be beyond our strength, though much may be beyond our present understanding of how to make that strength available.

—Newcomb.

February 26

We can at all times open our ears to either harmony or discord, for there is no environment yet discovered where either exists without the other. Through the science of adjustment we learn to relate ourselves pleasantly and helpfully to every individual and incident that comes into our lives. Impatience delays results, while ready acceptance hastens them.

–Newcomb.

February 27

Success is the expression of true individuality. None can bestow it on another. None can prevent or hinder. It must be won by each of us, and through the winning we accomplish our development. This is a simple creed, and one that never needs to be revised, as every step of progress furnishes fresh evidence of its truth.

–Newcomb.

February 28

All our difficulties are but tests of our powers. None of them are sufficient to explain our failures. All the good powers of the universe are drawn to our side in the day of battle, if we raise the banner of Truth. The only boon Truth asks is the opportunity of expression through our lips and lives, that *we* may receive her benediction.

–Newcomb.

March 1

We talk of love as an emotion, when we ought to recognize it as a principle that underlies the universe. Emotional love is but a faint suggestion of the great power, Love, whose sounding-line has never been fathomed. True love seeks nothing for itself, but the power of expression. Jealousy is the selfish clamor of unloving thought. It is a parody of love and always without excuse.

—Newcomb.

March 2

Truth has never known defeat, and in so far as we ally ourselves with truth, do we become invincible. No chains of circumstance can fetter the true man. He asks no odds of fortune, and in every hour of adversity he expresses power, and calmly awaits victory, knowing that it is sure to come.

–Newcomb.

March 3

It is the nature of happiness to radiate and enlarge its expression by finding others with whom it can share its joys. Goodness and happiness are really interchangeable terms. When we have succeeded in obtaining happiness for ourselves or others, we may be sure we have been gaining and bestowing both goodness and power.

—Newcomb.

March 4

The only trouble with many people is stagnation through depression. Their chief lack is momentum. A little more forceful motion would take them altogether away from their difficulties and diseases. They wear their yokes like oxen, because they do not realize the power in themselves. Let their realization be awakened, and their spiritual will aroused, and applied with its tremendous energy, and all bonds and obstructions will easily fall away.

—Newcomb.

March 5

We cannot play the chords of "success" upon an instrument relaxed by disappointment and discouragement. Through happiness you will be successful. There is no force so healing as the thrill of joy and gladness. There is no stimulant that is more speedy and thorough in its action. It is a natural tonic, and the entire system responds to its exhilarating vibrations.

—Newcomb.

March 6

Anything that arouses confidence in life, with a larger sense of its use and beauty, increases human energy and prepares the best conditions of success in all its undertakings. It is even better to build castles in the air, than to dwell in caves of gloom. The imagination is more worthily employed in picturing pleasant things than in brooding fears and entertaining dark forebodings.

–Newcomb.

March 7

If one has awakened to an understanding of the real, and a power of discernment of the artificial,—if he has developed the creative instincts of the soul,—he is no longer swept away by tides and currents he cannot control. In joy he finds his strength, and he lives in *today*. What have I to do with the yesterdays or the tomorrows of my life? My responsibility lies strictly in the present.

—Newcomb.

March 8

Why should I scatter and weaken my thought-forces by regretful recollections of the imperfect yesterday or anxious anticipation of the uncertain morrow? I will concentrate all my energy upon the passing hour, and thus will atonement be made for the past, and grace developed for the future. Today–*today* I live. The depression, the grief of yesterday is past. Today I will triumph. Tomorrow shall find me a victor!

–Newcomb.

March 9

We are so ready to magnify every trouble. We are so prone to make a burden of life. True life is an *ever-present* opportunity. It is not concerned with past or future. It is in the lowlands only that we suffer from the malaria of memory and fear, and our spiritual perceptions are bedimmed and paralyzed. Great souls need never be beggars of "circumstance" to manifest their quality. They are masters of all conditions.

—Newcomb.

March 10

Spiritual progress is never hindered by our duties or want of time. There can be no conflict between our aspirations, and our duties and responsibilities. Our most precious opportunities are often those disguised in tatters. They pass us by unrecognized, because we judge life by appearances instead of principles.

—Newcomb.

March 11

Life is always at its flood, though our realization may ebb and flow. It is only we who imagine the ebb, as we wade in the murky waters of a shallow experience, indulging in self-pity, and bemoaning our sufferings. If we cease our vain struggles and lamentations long enough to look away from the personal self, and recognize the spiritual self with its calm confidence of inexhaustible energies, we realize that life is going well with us after all.

—Newcomb.

March 12

We exhaust our strength in our impatience at our work, and the conditions that surround us. There is nothing that comes to us which we could not do easily with true adjustment, but we waste our forces in our worries. It is our leverage that is at fault. When that is changed, we will find the heaviest weights are easily raised.

–Newcomb.

March 13

The mechanism of our existence is simpler than we think. None of its cog-wheels are misplaced. If we only permit them to work into each other where they belong we will discover that there is no superfluous friction, and the adjustment of experience to need is truly marvelous.

—Newcomb.

March 14

Truth is never dependent to the least degree upon the personality of teachers. We must not imagine Truth will stand or fall by any personality. Telegraphy remains an accurate manifestation of electric science even though all the operators in the land be proven incompetent and unreliable.

—Newcomb.

March 15

When our suffering seems almost beyond endurance, we may always gain relief by making a bold "change of front." Instead of declaring, as we so often do in our mental anguish, "I can't stand it any longer," let us assert with St. Paul, "I glory in tribulation." "I take pleasure in infirmities." "I can endure all things." It raises the combative forces within us, and we push forward, and make a fresh start.

–Newcomb.

March 16

How vastly different a troubled question looks to us at noonday and at midnight. We flinch in the hours of darkness from a problem we can meet bravely when we are on our feet, and tinder the momentum of the noonday vigor. This is all the difference between negative and positive conditions. Let us remember this, when the experience comes to us. The question is the same. It depends on our attitude of mind to meet it.

—Newcomb.

March 17

Man can open wide all doors of receptiveness,—can throw down all walls and live in the open,—or he can shut himself up in the deepest dungeons of his personal life, and bar out every ray of sunlight. The sun is powerful indeed, but the delicate membrane of the human eyelid can exclude it when man so wills. Nothing is so blinding as the persistent thought of weakness.

—Newcomb.

March 18

By boldly and persistently changing our thought from the negative conditions of discouragement and suffering, to the positive conditions of strength and life, the very worst case of nervous prostration can be quickly overcome. Nature abounds in remedial power, and is always within our reach. Let us begin by *ceasing to oppose,* ceasing to *fight our troubles,* declaring their nonentity, and giving ear to the inner and divine self, whose voice we have learned to know.

–Newcomb.

March 19

When through being negative our body becomes sick, if we turn right about in our thought and become positive, we are by so doing accomplishing a positive molecular change. We have turned off the current of anxious thought. We have altered our polarity. We have accomplished with our troubles the same results that would follow to the iron filings grouped about the magnet if it should be suddenly demagnetized. The bits of iron fall away. They have nothing to which to cling.

—Newcomb.

March 20

If we would *loosen* our life we would always save it. Every hour of emergency will bring its own deliverance to him who waits with confidence. The fears and sufferings which we encounter in one place are left behind as we move on. Higher levels are always accessible. We need not struggle with any difficulty upon the plane where it appears. We must climb the spiritual hillsides. In other altitudes we will find the sunshine.

—Newcomb.

March 21

Love is the real power which rules our universe and weaves the warp and woof of life, throwing its shuttle with a wisdom and precision which seems marvelous to our half-opened eyes. All suffering comes from misdirected energy. A wholesome nature finds its pleasure in its work and turns the current of force into it, thereby accomplishing great results.

—Newcomb.

March 22

All error is the incomplete statement or manifestation of something real. It is a partial and imperfect inspiration, and speedily brings its own correction through the suffering it entails. The lesson of right expression is the most important we have to learn. Mind poisoning precedes blood poisoning. When we dwell in secret upon the thought of trouble, we expose ourselves to further dangers.

–Newcomb.

March 23

We too often hasten through the passing days with but scanty enjoyment or stolid endurance, looking hazily to some distant time for the fulfilment of desire. The best conditions for future happiness lie in the largest possible appreciation of the present. This is a truth we all admit, yet we spend our lives in following happiness as a phantom, and blinding ourselves to the present good.

—Newcomb.

March 24

We should never contend with a fear. It is a waste of time and effort, and as useless as to argue with hysteria. We need to establish firmly in our minds the thought of our sovereignty. We never fear that which we know we can control, and we are here for the purpose of learning the mastery of what we call Fate.

—Newcomb.

March 25

If we turn to the contemplation of the divine power we embody, *all* our fears will pass away like the shadows of the night. Fear is a mental mirage. It is an optical illusion—a refraction of certain lines and angles due to our mental atmospheric conditions, and to false lights that result in grotesque distortion of the real. Success is determined by our force of character and strength of resolution.

—Newcomb.

March 26

When life is disturbed by perpetual conflict, we may know that our method of campaigning is at fault. We have failed to direct our forces wisely. We have not understood and tested the resources upon which we could have drawn;—else our advance would have been less difficult. There is no greater source of weakness than to dwell upon the power of an adversary until our courage has been undermined.

—Newcomb

March 27

Many men persist in the conviction of their *inability*. It is the only thing in which they fully believe, and every obstacle they meet is met from this standpoint, and magnified by their erratic fancy and their feeble will. This is the worst possible form of cowardice, and the rankest kind of atheism.

–Newcomb.

March 28

The keenest pleasure we receive through our sense life is but the faintest suggestion of the gladness of the spirit. Instead of distrusting and condemning the sensuous nature and strangling its expressions, we should understand its spiritual correspondence. Spirit is altogether sensibility and knowledge.

–Newcomb.

March 29

To overcome disease or difficulty, we must strike a vibration higher or lower than the one prevailing on the plane of its manifestation. A nervous tension needs to be relaxed by striking a lower keynote. A depressed condition can be stimulated by a higher. Mind and matter are the wings upon which we rise to higher conditions through the guidance of the will. These factors must be balanced and adjusted to each other.

–Newcomb.

March 30

Search as diligently as we may, we will not discover in material things the key to satisfaction, or the answer to our perplexities. Spirit alone can solve our riddles, for the reason that we are spiritual beings. If we will brush the dust of selfishness from the lenses through which we look at life, we will find illumination for every emergency. Our spiritual vision will never be dimmed.

–Newcomb.

March 31

When we resent and resist our difficulties, we provide the most favorable mental soil for their rooting and growth. The germ which would have easily passed over us harmlessly finds lodgment and nurture in our minds, and rapidly externalizes itself upon our bodies. We suffer only because we fail to transmit the harmonies which crowd continually upon us, and would have their passage through us, if we would permit.

—Newcomb.

April 1

No vows of obedience are necessary except to the higher self through which God reveals himself. When we move forward with the will and the step of the conqueror, we leave far behind us all the hosts of difficulty that seemed to compass us about. Life is a succession of wonderful transformation scenes. Thought is the scene-shifter. Nothing is beyond its skill and power in the moments of its highest concentration.

—Newcomb.

April 2

There is great danger in constant dissatisfaction. Sooner or later it will involve the health or finances, or both, for it destroys the mental balance, and impairs the judgment. If we indulge ourselves in sadness or impatience we may be always sure our sin will find us out. Impatience opens the door to hysteria, anger, and insanity, which mark regular stages in the loss of self-control.

—Newcomb.

April 3

The powers of will and concentration are shown in vice and disease as well as in virtue and health. They manifest perversion of force, and not failure. Concentration is poise of mind rather than forced action. Repose of spirit is absolutely essential to the highest expression of power. We should neither dream through the day nor wake through the night,—in both these ways we scatter force.

—Newcomb.

April 4

The higher self knows no fear, and sees no obstacles. It passes everywhere unhurt. All difficulties change into walls of defense behind it. All power is the expression of knowledge. This is attained only through experience. As soon as we have gained adjustment to one situation, we encounter another, demanding the exercise of unused forces. Mortal life is not a dream, except to those who prefer to sleep.

—Newcomb.

April 5

There are always two voices sounding in our ears,—the voice of fear and the voice of confidence. One is the clamor of the senses, the other is the whispering of the higher self. If we listen to the first we are unnerved. If we give heed to the other, we develop power and become invincible.

—Newcomb.

April 6

When science has admitted that the atom is intelligent and indestructible, it has transmitted matter into mind, for we know of nothing else than mind that can make these claims. Matter offers the resistance necessary for demonstration of the superior power of mind. It is the substance that we were sent here to study, and to control.

–Newcomb.

April 7

There is no matter without motion. There is no motion without mind. Atoms and thoughts are alike magnetic, and through the selecting principle attract all other atoms and thoughts of the same vibration. Matter is mind at a slower rate of vibration,–mind is matter at a higher rate. Spirit is infinitely more rapid than either, and rules both.

–Newcomb.

April 8

We are absolutely the architects of our own fortunes, and should no longer seek to shelter ourselves behind the superstitions of "heredity" and "fate." Every man is a "*self-made* man." He builds the temple that his soul inhabits. Whatever its beauties or deformities, they are the manifestation of his own thought in the past,—even if that past has faded from his recollection.

—Newcomb.

April 9

Matter is the matrix of the mind. It receives the impress of thought and expresses it in form. When we have learned to live, we will find the body an organ of wondrous power, and never a clog or hindrance. A constant and buoyant gladness is the right expression of true life. Our health and fortunes suffer through our failure to recognize this and our opportunities, which wait on all sides for us to see and take hold of.

–Newcomb.

April 10

Nature feeds us on all sides. We draw our life through millions of pores, and give expression to it in diverse and wonderful ways. It is always our doubts that paralyze our energies. Power is the purpose of life. Imagination cannot outstrip the power of execution. Large conceptions of the soul's potencies speedily manifest themselves in material life. The present is as infinite as the past or future.

–Newcomb.

April 11

It is not conceit to realize and claim our spiritual powers. It is only the egotism of the personal man that ever doubts or denies them. We call ourselves practical when our actions appeal to the sense life, and their good results are felt, or heard, or seen. We are never truly practical except when we have learned to govern and apply our highest thought.

–Newcomb.

April 12

The first step toward freedom is right listening. The next step is right answering to our part in the song of life. If we hear truly we shall live truly. Nothing in life is of greater importance than that we should learn the law of harmony. We are so deafened by the tumult of discordant chords rising from the material man, that many have to be trained to hear even the *faintest sounds* of harmony.

—Newcomb.

April 13

The ear is a wonderful avenue of sense. More than eight thousand delicate nerves lead from it to the brain. As yet they are only partially developed. Many insects hear a lower vibration and some animals a higher one than reaches our mortal ears. Scientists tell us that a sound wave goes on forever. Through currents of sympathetic vibration the sounds to which we are attuned will reach our ears.

—Newcomb.

April 14

What makes the soul deaf to truth? What are the obstructions to right listening? Let us examine some of the laws of harmony. We often fail through *discouragement*. You should drop that word out of your life. Dissatisfaction with ourselves and our own lot dulls all sense of harmony. We moan at our vexations. Our atmosphere is full of morbid thoughts and fears of ill health. Shut your ears to these negative vibrations, and listen for the positive ones of gladness.

–Newcomb.

April 15

Discouragement results in pity for ourselves. This is a further cause of deafness. *Self-pity* is an opiate that benumbs the nerves of a higher consciousness. Why can we not take life as cheerily as the sailor takes his changeful voyage? Our ear is at fault because we are not teachable. We will not patiently listen to the truth. We do not believe in our capacity to hear it, or we are too indolent to try. The fault is all in ourselves.

—Newcomb.

April 16

Indecision is a note of inharmony. The more we listen to discordance the more the ear gets out of tune. If we have not reached a final decision in our own minds that we *can* be well and happy and prosperous,–if we are not yet quite sure that life is really good and sweet and joyous in itself, we are not likely to hear melodious tones.

–Newcomb.

April 17

The work of reconstruction begins with action of will. With confidence in life restored and a true purpose assured, we will soon find our hearing is enlarged. The sound waves change their character and pass from grave to gay. We hear and see according to our moods as long as we permit them to govern our lives.

–Newcomb.

April 18

If we do not find time to *live,* we shall very soon be forced to find time to die. Life administers severe rebukes to our impatience when we make it necessary. Nothing is more valuable than to learn how to wait cheerfully. It is a good evidence that we are answering life's song in notes of *power.* Power is expressed in positive conditions. We cannot afford to risk the negative. There is no danger to the *fearless* soul.

–Newcomb.

April 19

If we are capable of conceiving love it is because we ourselves are loving. We understand wisdom to the extent that we are wise. We believe in power because we have its possibilities within us. "The Lord is the strength of my life. Of whom shall I be afraid?" Power attracts power, as strong men enroll themselves under the banners of successful leaders.

–Newcomb.

April 20

The soul will never be satisfied with mediocrity. From every level it perceives another height towering above it, and pushes forward strong and buoyant in the spirit of conquest, and with no sense of weariness. We will answer life's song in a spirit of *service*. Service is the law of harmony as it is of love. It is in activity for others that we gain the largest freedom for ourselves.

–Newcomb.

April 21

We are never without our opportunities of service. Every opportunity brings with it its own power. Every sincere thought or act of helpfulness is an impulse of spiritual development. We think sometimes that it belongs to those who possess, to give. Possession *comes* through giving, and not giving through possession. The universal stores of God are open to every honest demand.

–Newcomb.

April 22

Responsibility and opportunity never exist apart. If we discover one we may know that the other is close at hand. When we have learned that every human being is a part of the harmony we very soon begin to know its laws. When we are ready to obey them the discords of life are ended. But before the soul is awakened, we cannot understand the meaning of existence. It is the soul alone that can interpret the vision.

—Newcomb.

April 23

Adown the centuries has come the voice of Him whom Christians call "the Master." Dogmatists and translators have combined to make His accents so fragmentary and disjointed as to at times mutilate His message. But out of all the babel of commentators we know today that the Nazarene's tones are so full of melody that when the ear of man has heard, his whole soul listens.

—Newcomb.

April 24

Jesus taught life as a science, speaking with authority. Now we really know for the first time that the law of love is the law of life, and that the golden rule is the most scientific proposition that has ever been submitted to a skeptical world. For centuries the discords of theology have deafened our ears to His ringing message, and dulled our brains to a true understanding. But now the true meaning is dawning in man's mind.

–Newcomb.

April 25

The law of harmony permits no note of selfishness. The Sermon on the Mount is a key to all the mysteries that surround us. We are beginning to faintly discern new notes in the great song as it is sung by human voices such as have not been heard for many centuries. By and by we shall hear the song of a larger life, and know the beauties of the astral harmonies. On planes yet unexplored we will apply the principles we are learning here.

–Newcomb.

April 26

No matter what ancestral trait has been reproduced, no matter what taint in the blood has shown itself anew, it can be wholly overcome in any individual life. It can be eradicated from the system when the soul has been aroused to its work. Man builds the temple of his soul, and he can change at will the colors or the texture of the thought with which he builds.

–Newcomb.

April 27

The New Thought teaches that all heredity, environment and interior conditions are controlled by the soul, and that man's life is not governed to the least degree by any outside circumstances. He simply responds to these as they touch the chords of sympathetic vibration within himself. It teaches him to live at the centre rather than the circumference of life—to live in the *now.*

—Newcomb.

April 28

"For it is God which worketh in you, both to *will* and to *do*." Neither illness nor poverty can result from the work of good. Good does not work meanly. It is the negative and weak condition of mind that produces ill health and poverty and all causes of suffering. Man's freedom is complete. No power in the universe compels him to be good. But when he has chosen good, he is invulnerable at every point, and "underneath are the Everlasting Arms."

–Newcomb.

April 29

Every activity should be a joy;— none a source of anxiety. We meet the requirements of the hour by directing our spiritual forces upon the work in hand. If we permit the Universal Will to guide us, and its power to act through us, we cannot fail to discern or improve any occasion of good service, or development.

—Newcomb.

April 30

It is useless to talk of spiritual truth to those who are hypnotized by prejudice. They simply cannot hear. The thought will fail to reach them, and result only in irritation. They must be awakened from their trance by some shock of life, before their ears are open. People that we *can* help will be attracted to us, and we will be led to others who can do *us* good. We can trust this law of spiritual attraction.

–Newcomb.

May 1

Every soul with honest, earnest purpose may be sure of finding the truth he seeks. It will often seem to be by paths and methods he would not have chosen. We have no reason, however, to fear failure in anything we are really called to do. We will find ourselves equipped for every work for which we are responsible.

–Newcomb.

May 2

All gymnastic apparatus are built in a way that the muscles of the body may meet *resistance.* The principle of muscular development is found in overcoming inertia. This is equally true of intellectual and spiritual development. We find the same law governs alike on all planes of life. All life demands expression, and there is no expression possible without resistance. What we call the trials of life are for this purpose.

–Newcomb.

May 3

If we could only understand that at *every* point of our lives "all is good," we could find no excuse for anxiety. It is always our atheism, or distrust of good, which is responsible for our trouble. God is imminent good. His spirit pervades the universe. The highest duty of each is self-development. It is the law of all true service and can never hinder, or cripple, or obstruct.

–Newcomb.

May 4

The highest duty of each human being is self-development, through service, but not *sacrifice.* We can trust our children and friends to God, and unfold our own lives to their highest possibilities, following the laws of growth and being we see in tree and flower. God is sufficient to all mankind, and every living creature must ultimately recognize this great truth.

–Newcomb.

May 5

Do not flatter yourself that you are the only agent for God's special work. He has thousands in reserve;–and if you fail to appreciate the privilege of the service, His work will not fail, only it will be your loss of opportunity,–not God's or that of others. You are never called to service without receiving sufficient strength to do it acceptably. God's service never requires loss of spiritual enjoyment. That is yours by right.

–Newcomb.

May 6

Do not be afraid of "self-seeking" on the highest lines, for when you have found your *real* self you have found God. For the *divine* self is the "Christ within," and by finding it you have fulfilled the very highest law of being. It is only when in harmony with this law that we are really "useful." God's service is too often thought to be a matter of bustling endeavor. First we must turn to Him and reflect Him, then what we do will be inspired.

–Newcomb.

May 7

We know that divine intelligence is never blind,—that divine power has no moments of weakness,—and that divine love is the mainspring of the universe. When we turn to God we should wait and listen, confident in the love that notes the fall of every sparrow. If we believe that God governs our lives, why cannot we rest assured that He governs equally those of our loved ones? Why should we disturb ourselves so wilfully?

—Newcomb.

May 8

Let us honestly admit that no distress can vibrate in a mind that is filled with God's harmonies,–a mind that is *persuaded* that God is neither blind, nor deaf, nor powerless, nor failing in love. We claim that the Supreme Government is universal, and extends to all worlds, and all times; therefore, we may be strong and confident in that knowledge.

–Newcomb.

May 9

A very common form of atheism is a distrust of self,–a want of confidence in the inner voice of one's own intelligence,–which is God within, and in one's own forces, which are but the expression of the Infinite. If God is without, He is equally within, else He does not fill all being. To doubt God outside of oneself has *always* been called atheism. It is atheism also then to distrust His reflection within.

–Newcomb.

May 10

Let us find God within ourselves, and we can then discern Him in all outer life. Let us trust our inner intuitions, and our powers to fulfil our purpose, knowing that in these is the law of the universal manifested to just that extent to which we open our minds for illumination, and let the divine work through us.

–Newcomb.

May 11

The test of courage can be made only in the presence of danger. Muscular strength is developed in the gymnasium, thus providing gradually conditions to overcome. Spiritual forces follow the same law. Why then should we moan and whine over every uncomfortable situation that life brings to us? Why not recognize it as the necessary problem of the hour, which God places before us to fulfil, in order to test our strength?

—Newcomb.

May 12

Our worries never fail to hinder our prosperity, though we do not yet understand the law that operates to retard or hasten. We are just beginning to recognize as a scientific fact, that "all action is in mind." All our life is "miracle." Up to now man has dealt mainly with the external expressions rather than the true causes. The science of thought is only just starting.

—Newcomb.

May 13

Receptiveness must come before illumination. Activity will surely follow. Growth is realization. If we do the thing that lies at hand, we cannot fail to find our place in the system of humanity. We will fulfil our destiny at every point. Life is an intelligent design. We cannot yet see the right side of the pattern that is being woven. But as Emerson says:–"We lie in the lap of an immense Intelligence."

–Newcomb.

May 14

We can endure quite calmly other people's worries because they do not belong to us through sympathetic vibration. Now, can we not reach the same position in relation to those we call our own? Can we not get outside of them and view them from an outside standpoint? If worry is not driven out of the blood, it is surely fatal, and only a matter of time. Killed by worry would be a truthful epitaph over multitudes of graves.

—Newcomb.

May 15

Absolute confidence in the wisdom and power of the good within us as being a reflection of the omnipotent wisdom and power of God, is necessary to the attainment of our purposes, and in order to make our lives effective and worth while. God *wants* us to be effective, and full of power and health and joy,–but He requires us to *grow into the power* of drawing these things to us.

–Newcomb.

May 16

Small annoyances are the seeds of disease. We cannot afford to entertain them. They are the bacteria and the germs that make serious disturbance in the system, and prepare the way for all derangements. They furnish the mental conditions which are manifested later in the blood, the tissues, and the organs, under various pathological names. Good thoughts are the only germicide. We must kill out resentment, anxiety and impatience. Health will follow.

–Newcomb.

May 17

Every thought that holds us even in the slightest degree to either anticipation or regret, hinders to some extent the realization of our present good. It limits freedom. Life is in the present tense. Its significant name is "being." The problem at hand is the one we are expected to solve,—we cannot see the nature of those we must meet in the future. The wisdom with which we deal with the present, largely influences all that comes later.

—Newcomb.

May 18

Let us waste no time in the sentimentalism of self-pity, but search with earnest purpose for the *meaning* of the hour, responding boldly to its challenge. Sympathetic vibration is the key of life. Every experience is limited by its responsive chords. Nothing can reach us from *without*, except as it awakens vibrations *within*. This is equally true of joy and sorrow.

–Newcomb.

May 19

We cannot build until we have laid foundation stones. We acid to our foundations every time we meet our difficulties well, however insignificant they may be. This is the way we fit ourselves for larger work in the emergencies and opportunities of life. Let us overcome vexation of all kinds. Let us be always tranquil and serene in every provocation. It is possible to the *great* soul.

—Newcomb.

May 20

Passive resentment to people and events is perhaps more subtle and injurious than open protest. We do not require resignation; that is only a masked vice. We want cheerful and bold acceptance of the problem. By this alone will we ever overcome and prepare the pleasanter conditions we desire. Every unpleasant thought must be immediately crushed out, and thrown away. We cannot permit it to produce a mental jar, or interrupt our spiritual progress.

—Newcomb.

May 21

To be receptive to harmonious thought, and to reject all that is discordant is the test of spiritual will. Let us learn to forget an injury. It is the only true forgiveness. To forgive is to forego, and to forego includes forgetfulness. In the same way we forget all trouble. Our recollections cause our mental inflammations and congestions. Real forgiveness does not assert "I can never forget."

–Newcomb.

May 22

Regret is self-resentment. Regrets would fade as we grow if we did not weave them into a hair shirt to wear against our skin. Nature is quick to wipe out all unpleasant sensations, and retain only what is agreeable in life. Our penances are self-imposed. We gain from them a certain gratification. They turn our thoughts inward and backward, when we ought to turn them outward, and concentrate them on the *present*.

—Newcomb.

May 23

All fear includes resentment,—we resent what we fear, and will discover it in honest analysis. Perfect love will cast it out. Regret and resentment bind upon us heavy burdens, from which we should cut loose. When we have cast off the remembrance of our troubles, we are no longer distressed by the power of association. Regret and resentment vanish. A new life and buoyancy come to us. The sunshine seems brighter. We are glad to be alive.

—Newcomb.

May 24

We overlook the dangers of annoyance,—depression, mortification, disappointment, indignation; as long as these impulses tincture our mind to the slightest degree we suffer unrest and fear. We dwell too much upon the thought of consequences,—"What will be the result of this act,—this word,—this letter? How will it be regarded?" We forget that if our purpose is truly wise and righteous, its fruit must be eventually good, in the nature of things.

—Newcomb.

May 25

If we follow the dictates of our better selves, let us stoutly refuse to be alarmed as to the results, though the whole world should disapprove. Let us trust to the soul's intelligence. The good within us is our judge. Perfect peace is the touch-stone of true living, and it abides with those whose minds are "stayed on good."

–Newcomb.

May 26

If we admit that God is love, it follows of necessity that all is good, if we include also a belief in the absolute sovereignty of God. Everything that Supreme Love asks of us is a perfect response, and *every* life is being educated with that end in view, at *every* instance of its existence. May we not then safely claim that nothing can limit the good that comes to us *except our own lack of recognition*?

—Newcomb.

May 27

It has been wisely said, "There are no penalties to virtue." If we suffer through another it must be because of some responsive chord within ourselves which is not well attuned. When we are spiritually sound, no thought, or word, or act that is discordant can arouse vibrations of pain. Nature's work is not so incomplete. It cushions us against all discord from without, and responds only when kindred chords are touched in the same key.

–Newcomb.

May 28

We have absolute control of our own instrument, its harmonies and discords. The same law that protects us from needless suffering produces in us the reaction of every evil thought directed towards another. We get no satisfaction in hammering material in which there is no responsive vibration. When we direct an unkind thought upon another and it finds no lodgment, the whole force of it returns upon ourselves, while the other is unhurt.

–Newcomb.

May 29

Cannot we see the folly of all indulgence in petty nagging, and malice, and resentment, which can only poison our own lives and bring suffering to ourselves? "The ways of Wisdom are ways of pleasantness, and all her paths are peace."

–Newcomb.

May 30

Congestion and inflammation are not possible when the soul is truly poised. Such symptoms indicate deficiency in circulation, due to the irritation of some fear or anxiety. Fear cannot exist when the soul is poised rightly. None can bestow upon us, and none can draw from us except according to the spiritual law of our own centres. This is always seeking to establish equilibrium of forces. We receive through giving and not through self-seeking. Relax the selfish thought, and trouble disappears.

—Newcomb.

May 31

We look too far afield for God. We do not need to take a telescope or microscope for what is closer than the nearest fellow-creature,—nearer than the air we breathe, or the food we eat. We have only to become receptive and ask for guidance, and God manifests Himself through our acts, and the wisdom of our decisions. "In Him we live, and move, and have our being." This is literally true, and the soul that ponders upon it will receive illumination.

—Newcomb.

June 1

We are often told that "thoughts are things." This is only a partial statement. Thoughts are living entities. They can often materialize if the concentration is sufficiently persistent. Let us realize this fact. Disease results primarily from thought. Health cannot be restored when thoughts are discordant. Of all the enervating influences of thought, *self-pity* is the most insidious. Until it is ruthlessly uprooted the body will sicken. It is a concentrated selfishness.

—Newcomb.

June 2

What is the reason that one day will appear beautiful to one person and dreary to another? Is it not all in the way the mind regards it? We send out discord, and in return the wind seems harsh and chill to us, and the sunshine has no warmth to it. We radiate peace, and all the woods and the fields send back to us a vibrating response. The winds are invigorating and the sunshine glorious. The difference is in the mind.

–Newcomb.

June 3

We fear to trust our wings. We plume and flutter them, but dare not throw our weight upon them. We cling too often to the perch, and excuse our timidity by saying we are "chained by circumstances." Yet there is the great buoyant atmosphere enfolding us, and our spiritual pinions are strong. Courage is what we lack. Demand joy, and peace and goodness, and blessings, and they will come to you—if only you have faith and patience and a cheerful outlook.

—Newcomb.

June 4

There is no such thing as "science" and "religion" taken separately. Science is true knowledge. All true knowledge is divine, and relates us to the infinite through the understanding. Consequently all true science comprehends religion, and genuine religion *must* be scientific. There can be no antagonism between spirit and matter. We find in matter the manifestation of spirit. The "conflict" of life resolves itself into the problems of life, which we are here to overcome.

–Newcomb.

June 5

Beware of wasting our opportunities. If we fail to respond nobly to any of the demands of our daily life, we involve ourselves in still more trying conditions. Nature never over-estimates our capacity, and never sets for us a harder problem than we can solve. If we are not satisfied with our conditions, we must change our thought. Our thought vibrations will certainly carry us just where we belong, as unerringly as water finds its level.

—Newcomb.

June 6

Higher spiritual atmospheres are always accessible to those who *desire* to inhale them. Every soul surrounds itself with its own atmosphere. In the name of science and of the eternal equities we deny hereditary limitations. We also deny that any life can be enslaved by its environment.

–Newcomb.

June 7

The principle of personal responsibility is the chief corner-stone of all spiritual work. We can build nothing of value or stability in our lives till we have accepted this fundamental truth. Whatever we are, or wherever we are, is the result of our spiritual choice, whether made consciously or unconsciously. The spirit knows what problems it is necessary for us to solve in order to grow into a clearer atmosphere.

–Newcomb.

June 8

In our spiritual nature we are like automatic valves. As long as we open ourselves to the lower motive and indulgence, we close ourselves to the higher by that very impulse. When we close the lower we open the higher. The choice is always ours.

–Newcomb.

June 9

We do not often realize the power of sounds in words. Every word spoken by human lips carries with it in the utterance a concentration of hypnotic force applied through its vibrations. These vibrations meet with a response from every mind attuned to a sympathetic key. There is no word in any language without this vibratory power. The words we use so lightly are possessed of truly magic powers to him who knows how to use them.

—Newcomb.

June 10

In the science of mind it is an essential help to right development to make the air about us vibrant with such words as "freedom," – "truth," – "health," – "love," – "success," – "wisdom," – "opulence." A wealth of such words spoken morning and night is a mental medicine-chest of incalculable value. It tunes the spirit to the right key. Insensibly we become positive and effective through their influence.

–Newcomb.

June 11

If in any hour we feel disturbed, we know our vibration must be changed. Here then is our remedy for restlessness. We control our vibratory life through thought. If we take up a new thought, we find the entire system responds to the change, and attunes itself to the new keynote. Say "Peace–Be still" over a number of times, and insensibly the body relaxes and the nerves are soothed. We become receptive to harmony, and discord melts away from us.

–Newcomb.

June 12

"To take no anxious thought for the morrow" is to focus our highest power on today, and know that we have spiritual reserves for *all* contingencies of life. We must learn that life is something of the present moment, and that it is a serious loss of power, as well as happiness, to do everything with a view to being "prepared for the worst," upon which so many pride themselves.

–Newcomb.

June 13

Environment may color but it never molds the character. It gives nothing more than a veneering, and the natural wood will show through sooner or later. Its grain cannot be concealed. The hero is not hidden in the slums. The scoundrel cannot hide himself amid luxurious surroundings. Each will work out his own true character in spite of birth and position. We are *creators* of circumstance, not its creatures.

—Newcomb.

June 14

Truth is something infinitely beyond our petty personalities and egotistical limitations. It comes in the silence into every heart that it finds open for its reception,—or rather it opens gently our heavy eyelids to perceive that we live amid its glories and in its very courts,—that it broods and permeates us like the very atmosphere we breathe,—this "light that never shone on land or sea."

—Newcomb.

June 15

Light is positive and radiates. Darkness is negative and absorbs. One is powerful and the other powerless. So with good and evil. We underestimate the *power* of good. We exaggerate the power of evil. Evil is the weakest thing in life, and contrary to all the tides and currents of the universe. Good has all the forces of the Infinite behind it. Its *power is incalculable.* It never fails.

–Newcomb.

June 16

Life is flexible and is shaped by our thoughts. Man is at the same time a pupil and an architect. Let him accept the truth that all things work together for good, and he will find abundant confirmation of it in his daily experience. When we humor our weaknesses, they force themselves continually upon our attention, like spoiled children. When we assert our mastery of ourselves and compel its recognition, we stand secure in our sovereign rights.

–Newcomb.

June 17

If we were to dwell long upon the fact that our bodies live under a constant atmospheric pressure of fifteen pounds to the square inch, we should feel crushed and suffocated. Why do we not suffer? Because the resisting power of the atmosphere within is always equal to the pressure from without. So in our life of daily responsibility. When we consider only the care that comes from without we feel the weight of the pressure. When we remember we live in good we know that the Universal Force can never fail us. It is within and without.

—Newcomb.

June 18

Life itself inflicts no pain upon us. All suffering comes from within. It proceeds from the inharmonious conditions of our own souls. No pang can endure beyond the moment when we have restored harmonious vibrations to the mind,—have adjusted our own relations to people and events. The necessary and infallible result of mental harmony is health of body, opulence of environment, and love of friends.

—Newcomb.

June 19

Love is the keynote of life. Its harmonies are sublime. It is a magnet of irresistible power which draws to us all things desirable. Destiny there surely is,—but it is the consequence of an inner cause. It is not the arbitrary government of the great intelligence,—God. Our destiny will inevitably lead us to Him and His immutable laws, but we have our choice as to when we will turn our hearts to Him. If we remain in the darkness the fault is ours.

—Newcomb.

June 20

Any day of life, any moment of time, may be made the starting point of success. Let us "rejoice as a strong man to run a race." "And should the twilight darken into night, and sorrow grow to anguish, be thou strong,–thou art in God, and nothing can go wrong which a fresh life-pulse cannot set aright:– That thou dost know the darkness *proves the light.*"

–Newcomb.

June 21

We do not admit limitations as of old. It has instead become an axiom that any purpose man is capable of forming, he is capable of carrying to fulfilment. We know that the only crown we will ever receive is the crown of character, and that it is ours as soon as we choose to wear it. We need not wait for supernatural opportunities or gifts. Our life here amply provides us with every chance to "grow in grace."

—Newcomb.

June 22

We too often call ourselves and one another "prisoners of poverty," "creatures of circumstances," "victims of injustice or disease." All our prisons are mental. Truth gives us the pass-key to all doors,–the control of all environment,–deliverance from all injustice and disease. Freedom comes only through full recognition and admission of truth.

–Newcomb.

June 23

"In thy *presence* is fulness of joy." This should give us the keynote of existence. We expect the joy as a result of what we call "success." We think we can be happy when our purpose is accomplished. Let us reverse our methods, and expect the "success" as the result of the joyful mind in which we live. Let us look for the fulfilment of our purpose, because of the happiness in which we work. A joyful spirit radiates a clear atmosphere in which we see afar; an anxious mind befogs us.

–Newcomb.

June 24

There are no conditions of life possible when we need be joyless after we have learned life's meaning, and opened our eyes to the presence of the everlasting good in which we live. We are only just beginning to open our eyes to the fact that poverty and disease spring from the same cause, and are subject to the same remedy. Cause and remedy are within the individual himself, and proceed from a condition of mind. We draw poverty and disease to us through the negative currents.

–Newcomb.

June 25

Environment and fortune are simply indications of our state of mind. These can be changed by setting up for ourselves new standards, and making fresh statements of the principles of life. Discord cannot result from the right interpretation of the notes of a master in harmony. Disease and poverty are not expressions of an enlightened mind.

–Newcomb.

June 26

A feverish mind is not a good magnet. The point of equilibrium is the beginning of success, for it is at that point we realize that material wealth is not in itself an element of happiness. Unhappiness comes always from a failure to discern the right relation of things. Unhappiness is of the mind and is governed from within. When this lesson has been learned, we have reached a point of independence never known by us before. Wealth is now our servant, not our master.

–Newcomb.

June 27

We now know the meaning of the words:– "the kingdom of God is within." We have been always expecting it from without. There is no real possession possible until after we have attained self-possession. When this has been accomplished we will know that we cannot fail to win or to hold anything belonging to us, and life will manifest affluence.

–Newcomb.

June 28

We are neither the creature nor the slave of circumstances, though we have been taught to think so. Circumstances have their rise within us,–*always*. There are reactionary conditions which hold us to our orbits till we have consciously become their master by the recognition of our own divine intelligence and power.

–Newcomb.

June 29

Let us enlarge our world by expanding ourselves. All mankind has endless opportunity. Our limitations are always those we make ourselves. Life itself has no bounds, no walls, no doors. It is free to all. Every individual has his own particular vibration which affects his every act and determines the method in all his works. Each one draws to himself corresponding vibrations whether of joy or sorrow, poverty or opulence, love or hate.

—Newcomb.

June 30

True life is perfect freedom,– perfect equity. All our suffering and deprivation come from our interior conditions. All the great influences and forces of nature work for the accomplishment of our highest good. "Let a man then know his worth and keep things under his feet." The Bible continually is urging man to recognize his divinity. We are only just beginning to realize the tremendous power that comes with the recognition.

–Newcomb.

July 1

"Neither be ye of doubtful mind" contains a whole volume on practical scientific philosophy. Spiritual health is a condition of perfect equanimity, freed from all uncertainty, anxiety, and impatience. It perceives the Eternal Equities. It is the normal condition of the soul, *here* and *now*. It is the "heaven within."

–Newcomb.

July 2

In the effort to develop the spiritual nature, remember that man is a triune creature. Our *three* natures must be symmetrically unfolded before we can attune ourselves to spiritual harmonies. Man the animal is one with man the intellect and man the spirit. All is divine. There is no lower and no higher where there is perfect symmetry in God's marvelous kingdom.

–Newcomb.

July 3

A higher spiritual development discloses to us that the tides and currents of human life move with an irresistible power and always in the right direction. To gain the best results we have only to put ourselves fearlessly in the stream and move in harmony with spiritual law. We can never obstruct, but we may be, through our own act, in such uncomfortable relations to these tides and currents that we suffer discord in ourselves.

–Newcomb.

July 4

No true work can ever be accomplished until purposed and directed by the spiritual will. Such work can never fail. Its demonstration will be prompt and thorough when we have made it possible through harmony of thought. The spiritual will is the divine. We need only allow its powerful currents to flow through us. When we have adjusted our lives to right purposes every experience will be transmitted into wisdom.

–Newcomb.

July 5

The vital matter for us is the character of our thought life and the purity of our purpose. If these are true, all circumstances and environments will quickly respond and adjust themselves harmoniously. We need not fear to aim at the highest good for ourselves and others, but we must be confident of its attainment, without reserve or limitation. If we do not obstruct our spiritual vision with worries, doubts, depression, impatience, there is no instant of life when our perceptions will be dim.

—Newcomb.

July 6

When we remember the tireless energy of the universal life of which we are a part, we know that it can never fail us. We need not carry the world upon our shoulders. If we have a true understanding of life, we are never wearied. Good is infinite energy, and in good we live. It is also infinite repose. In spiritual chemistry "being" is the true primate; "doing" is its manifestation.

–Newcomb.

July 7

If "being" in us is symmetrical, we will never be distressed about the lack of opportunities in doing. We will never falter.

"Thou hast the truth,
Thou hast the life within thee,
It shall guide aright.
Trust then thy promptings day by day
And safely they shall lead the way."

–Newcomb.

July 8

Life is an experience of ripening. The green fruit has but small resemblance to that which is matured. Our judgments of each other are necessarily imperfect, as our experience and knowledge of any human life is very limited. As our horizon widens we become more charitable and patient. We learn to understand the beauty of that Hind proverb, "To know all is to forgive all."

–Newcomb.

July 9

The greatest service one can render: another is to believe in him. Let us persistently refuse to take each other seriously when we express anything but our best; to think meanly of another tends to lower his tone and relax his hold upon himself. It is a great loss to a man to forfeit even for a moment his right to think well of himself.

—Newcomb.

July 10

In spite of our seeming failures and the bitter disappointments of our purposes, we will none of us find at the last that our life was altogether fruitless; many things of which we thought but little will bring to us the greatest satisfaction. He who has learned a single letter of the alphabet has not entirely wasted his opportunities. Let us value the passing hour and concentrate on it all our forces.

–Newcomb.

July 11

Let us move on, and step out boldly, though it be into the night, and we can scarcely see the way. A higher Intelligence than the mortal sees the road before us. We do not have to strive for good, but only to go forward and possess it. Good awaits us at every step. Nothing but fear can blind us.

–Newcomb.

July 12

When a man has "come to his own" in the recognition of his divinity he counts all "tribulation" a cheap price to pay for the discovery. Let us teach the personal man that his freedom day has arrived when he has willingly recognized the wisdom of his spiritual self, and become his own loyal comrade and associate. The sorest experience of life becomes indifferent to us when we have had a moment of revelation.

–Newcomb.

July 13

Nothing but our personal choice demands that we shall respond to false vibrations. We have the power to strike and hold any keynote at will. We need not come into another's discord,—or be distressed that it exists. We are surely not responsible that our neighbor has no ear for music. It is important only for each one to see to it that his own notes should sound out loud and clear.

—Newcomb.

July 14

It may not be our privilege to cast out the mote from our neighbor's eye. We are never prevented from pulling the beam out of our own eye. It is a good rule of conduct never to excuse oneself, or to accuse another. We are not responsible for the opinion of others, regarding either our own conduct or the problems of life.

–Newcomb.

July 15

We hang to our troubles. They neither seek nor cling to us except as we attract and hold them. When we change the vibration that drew them, they drop off, and we are at peace again. It is our own hand that is on the lever – *always.* The force that has seemed to drive us backward, will drive us forward with equal power,–if we will *change its application.*

–Newcomb.

July 16

We are fitted to meet every responsibility that belongs to us. Let us greet it with cordial welcome and calm confidence in both our purpose and ability. It is for this we are here. We sometimes have the power of action, but by our selfishness are blinded to our opportunities and the responsibilities that come with them. Since all real action is in mind and that is within our own domain, we can *always* adjust ourselves to people, events and environment.

–Newcomb.

July 17

Skill in the science of living demands of us a prompt and cheerful adaptation of ourselves to existing conditions. This is always a mental process. It is afterwards externalized in a satisfactory environment. The first condition of dominating a difficulty is to dismiss all antagonism to persons and events. We are then prepared to consider the question calmly—as we would weigh a mathematical proposition.

—Newcomb.

July 18

Pain indicates a need of adjustment. We have seen that all experience that comes to us we have ourselves invited,—consciously or unconsciously,—that it brings a lesson to be learned and so is valuable and friendly. Wisdom welcomes all experience as necessary education. The comfort or discomfort of it is a minor matter. No problem can come into any life which is not for that life to solve.

—Newcomb.

July 19

It behooves us to exercise our God-given creative energy to uprear and invoke pure ideals, and to arrange them after the divine plan. It is not merely a sentiment, but a statement of scientific exactitude that when we dwell in and link ourselves to the infinite strength, we have no relations with weakness, evil and disorder.

–H. Wood.

July 20

Our weak and negative states leave us open to "take on" outside prevailing conditions. If any particular order of disease or infirmity is prevalent, we open the gate,–or rather it is already open,–and it walks in, and we coddle and entertain it. We are shaken with the wind and float with the current, because we present the negative rather than the positive poles of our nature.

–H. Wood.

July 21

The doctrine of "natural depravity" gives men a decided impetus in that direction. On the contrary if they can be induced to look at and magnify the divine within them, they are not only on the road to salvation, but are saved. Every mental and spiritual quality radiates and propagates itself, and brings its outward correspondences into action.

–H. Wood.

July 22

Thought waves are like musical vibrations. If certain strings of a piano are struck, the corresponding notes of other pianos near-by are stirred into action. Deep calls to deep, and like unto like. One who regards soundness as normal and to be expected, sheds it broadcast, and his very presence will strengthen and uplift. The spiritually developed mind carries with it a veritable halo, and soothes and restores when any friction exists.

–H. Wood.

July 23

Isaiah showed a profound knowledge of higher law when he declared: "They that wait upon the Lord shall renew their strength; they shall mount up with wings as eagles; they shall run and not be weary; they shall walk and not faint." To "wait upon the Lord" is to conform to divine methods and ideals.

–H. Wood.

July 24

The divine that is in you is *you*. The deific incarnation in Jesus is not lowered or disparaged, but all humanity, in varying degrees of unfoldment, is lifted towards it. In addressing our friend we should hold his *true* self in our consciousness, for by appealing to that we help it into manifestation.

–H. Wood.

July 25

"As in Adam all die, so in Christ shall all be made alive." The Adamic condition is error and carnality, which leads to death; and this death is not physical dissolution but the extinguishment of the good. In Christ all are made "alive"; that is, the Christly consciousness is life, health and peace, and this causes all seeming opposites to vanish. A positively developed spiritual nature is invulnerable to any "evil" thing known in the whole universe of God.

—H. Wood.

July 26

Constant solicitude regarding the physical welfare of our near friends and the fear that something adverse may befall them, starts currents that actually tend toward that which is feared. The attitude of perfect trust in the growing and ripening good of all things, is only reached as the spiritual standpoint is gained. The pure optimistic ideals which the higher evolution shows to be true and scientific, are the great saving element to humanity.

–H. Wood.

July 27

It is important for every one who is trying personally to apply these principles, to understand that all progress is vibratory and uneven. The higher standpoint is only reached through a long series of "ups and downs"—but no one who is capable of receiving any revelation of truth can be content to remain stationary for a time, and then retrograde,—they *must* push forward to greater revelation. What we gain of truth is ours, and will never be taken away from us.

—H. Wood.

July 28

If we individually think of the path that we follow as one upon which there are hindrances to our advancement, we make a law of limitation for ourselves. We find that if we expect difficulties everywhere, we shall encounter them. We see that our own obstructing thought makes obstructions for us.

God's way for us is a way of peace, joy, and success. If we continue in this way we are sure to abide in all these. We find that we are not in bondage to the beliefs of the past, beliefs in limitation, beliefs that would bind us to adverse conditions.

—Unity Daily Word.

July 29

As a man listens to the voice within, the outer chorus of discordant noises is hushed, and then come peace and harmony. This is the Christ principle,–"The way, the truth, and the life." Man's way to find God, and all God-like wholeness, is through the Christ in himself. If life were ever inspired it should be inspired now, for the Christ spirit and quality are as truly living as when incarnate in Jesus of Nazareth.

–H. Wood.

July 30

The Master said, "No man cometh unto the Father but by me," that is, through the Christ principle or quality within. Every human child of God possesses the divine germ, and with its enfoldment there come all potency and possibility. When the soul of man is stirred to attain a larger truth, his one aspiration should be to be filled with a deeper faith. Truth and faith pour into the soul that is held open to receive them like sunshine.

–H. Wood.

July 31

Our highest privilege and office is to be channels through which the divine life shall flow out to invigorate and inspire. The essence of salvation and of true healing is the death of selfishness. Giving out, or ministration, is the great and highest law, divine and human. Thought sent out in loving waves never returns void. It has a positive healing influence both on sender and recipient.

–H. Wood.

August 1

The color and tone of mentality come out in every form and feature. It is infallible law that we show forth, and *are,* the total composite of past thinking. Let us put away pride, and admit that all primary causation is from *within.* We charge our ills to the weather, work, draughts, contagion, etc. These may be *occasions,* but our *receptivity* is the primary and real cause.

—H. Wood.

August 2

Faith is absolutely essential. We must believe or we will never move. Doubt and unbelief end in stagnation and death. Will is life. The illumined will is the divine energy, or God in us. It is the manifestation of the Eternal Will. Nothing can withstand its energy. It takes hold upon forces that are infinite. Doubt is disintegration. It is leaden, nerveless and cowardly. It leads into the "slough of despond."

—H. Wood.

August 3

Life is richer, love stronger, truth more beautiful, nature fairer, music sweeter, art diviner, than we have ever dreamed. It is according to our capacity that we understand these things. God is infinitely better than we have power to imagine. As yet we can only receive a faint spark of His glory. But as we develop we will be able to receive more, and ever more and more. His glory and power are limitless,–and his loving compassion ever present.

–H. Wood.

August 4

Thought always seeks embodiment. The thought of the engineer materializes in the completed engine, and that of the architect in the finished building. Both of these thought-forms will outlast their external expression, because they are built of more durable material. Every conceivable force and phenomenon, when traced back, has for its original basis *mind in operation;* and this activity is regular, orderly, and to be relied upon.

–H. Wood.

August 5

Simply to live is a wonderful privilege in itself, and it should be a constant joy. But to *what* are you alive? Is it merely to a daily routine, a conventional worldly round? How much do you really live outside of your chosen profession or occupation? Are you alive to ideals, and the higher consciousness and in vital touch with the unseen? Life can be rich, powerful, beneficent *today*. You must kindle new energy, and *really live*.

–H. Wood.

August 6

The power of the higher life and consciousness can be most effectively acquired by what is known as "going into the silence." No amount of intellectual or scholastic attainment can reveal that which comes only through aspiration, inner perception and feeling. By a sincere and persistent effort, one may abstract himself from material environment, and make his spiritual nature receptive, and God will flood every waiting apartment. This "still small voice" becomes audible to the inner hearing.

–H. Wood.

August 7

Everything that is distorted in mind carries its solidified crookedness into the body, and the process of straightening it out causes pain and friction. In proportion as man's mind and spirit are in the ascendant, his corporal structure will not be open to every discordant wave that is wafted toward him in the sensuous atmosphere.

–H. Wood.

August 8

Only "eternal vigilance" and constant thought consecration will keep one from being cast down by the lower currents of our mental environment. We rarely get more than we positively expect. It is well not to limit what we ask of life. If we live in harmony and by the Spirit, all that is good will come to us through vibratory attraction. This is a law of the universe.

–H. Wood.

August 9

Nothing above the commonplace can be made perfectly rational to a sluggish and unbelieving mind. The strong and united testimony of others should make us willing to have faith in some things that we may not as yet understand. It all depends on the progress we make towards a clearer spiritual vision as to our capacity to understand even the first glimmerings of truth. We reach it through thought and aspiration and *desire* to learn.

–H. Wood.

August 10

When we are open to truth on all sides, we work with perseverance and earnestness. We sometimes grow beyond our friends. Our family may be antagonistic to our beliefs. Do not think of what you could do if they were different, but accept them as they are, and live above their power to annoy you. It *can be done.* "Live what you believe, and you will know. You will get your illumination. You cannot learn for another. Indifference to conditions and the opinions of others gives poise."

—K. Newcomb.

August 11

Anything which subordinates the soul, and prevents a man from taking all that belongs to him as a free spirit in a beneficent world,—any mistaken sense of humility or self-suppression, has a harmful effect upon the whole life, and is evidently as far from a normal attitude as strong self-conceit. If one constantly feels promptings to do good and suppresses them, a reaction is sure to follow.

—Dresser.

August 12

We know, when on one hand, a man's soul speaks through his words, and when, on the other, he says one thing with his lips and thinks another, thereby trying to conceal his soul. The whole being speaks through a perfectly genuine act, through truly ethical conduct. We mean something genuine, something honest, appealing and *true,* bespeaking that indefinable thing called "personality." It is that which endears one to those who give us this exhilarating uplift, which is really a reflection of God.

—Dresser.

August 13

To some it seems impossible that the world could have been better than it is. Others hold that life could not have been worse. All conclusions and all ideals are relative to the state of development. For all men life is some sort of adjustment between inner and outer conditions. To discover that life moves *forward,* and each of us suffers or rejoices according to our relation to it, is perhaps the chief need to master.

–Dresser.

August 14

Probably the majority of men would agree that the highest aim of life is the full development of the soul. It is character that avails. If we are cast about by every wind that blows it is because we lack the repose that character brings. And to possess character is in some degree all that is asked of us, for when it is developed to a certain height the whole being is illumined and spiritualized.

—Dresser.

August 15

Our deepest life is a continuous incoming of renewing, sustaining power, welling up from the heart of the universe into the spirit of man,—a continuous divine communication engaged in the rearing of a soul. The deepest self is not physical, nor even intellectual; it is spiritual. We are spirits *now*, -in germ it may be; but in so far as we are conscious of our nearness to God, that consciousness will never be broken.

—Dresser.

August 16

Man is not a body with a soul, but a soul or spirit, which in every well-poised person is master of the body, and of the powers of thought and action. Want of charity, continued fault-finding, jealousy, insincerity, all these narrow the soul. Love of the truer sort, broad thinking, happiness, open-heartedness develop it. Sacrifice of individuality to the control of a stronger mind suppresses the soul.

—Dresser.

August 17

It is well to consider wherein we are held down by people and circumstances, and to discover how we are cramping our souls. The soul should be master, and the powers of thought and activity should be free. Do we not yield part of our manhood or womanhood when we worry,—when we give way to continued grief or discouragement? On the other hand the knowledge that we are living, growing spirits, who use the body as an instrument and control it by thought, this brings freedom.

—Dresser.

August 18

We have all experienced those calmer moments when we quietly faced our fears, our doubts, and our wavering opinions, and as calmly dismissed them, henceforth powerless because we saw their utter absurdity. Half the battle is won when we discover our error, and realize the possibilities of the soul. We are then at once masters of the situation. We then discover our inner centre, and become poised, and calm in eternal peace.

—Dresser.

August 19

When we realize our relationship to eternal power, the mind changes, and brings all things round to correspond to our deep desire. The ideal of daily conduct is to maintain this inward repose, to keep it steadily and persistently in view, to regain it when we lose it, to seek it when we need help, to have a calm centre within which is never disturbed, come what may,—a never-yielding citadel of the higher self.

—Dresser.

August 20

The soul must learn what it is, and why it is here. It must gain this knowledge by actual experience in order to learn the value of development,—in order to learn that there is an imminent wisdom, a love, that is equal to all occasions. It struggles upward and forward to completion.. It is ever trying to come forth and express itself, and when man comes to consciousness of what it means to develop the soul, and of the divine trend of his personal life, he no longer resists this deep moving.

—Dresser.

August 21

With deeper consciousness comes readjustment to life and more spiritual freedom. The soul finds better expression through the body, not in some future existence, but *here* and *now.* If anything is purposeful in the universe then, it is the life of man, as it passes from stage to stage in its progressive experience, unfolding and giving to the light the divinity involved in its very being.

—Dresser.

August 22

When man comes to the knowledge that the divine spark is within him, he gains poise and strength to pass through any experience without fear that it may prove too hard. When he is conscious that his spirit dwells with God, he need never fear any permanent harm. He is able to free himself rapidly from all that would hold him down

—Dresser.

August 23

People disturb us. They sap our vitality from us,—demanding all our force and patience. Be watchful as we may they pile upon us their conditions of fear, and their atmosphere of despondency. We find ourselves responding to it. We imagine ourselves ill-used, misunderstood, and wronged. Our faith is tested to the utmost, and we are pushed to the wall. In such cases we must regain our poise by the realization of the power that is ever within us. Find your centre. Learn to know your home in God.

—Dresser.

August 24

To know that everything we need is within, *here* and *now*,–this is poise. Realization teaches through actual communion with it, that there is an Omnipresent Spirit to whom we may turn at any moment and in any place, of whom our being partakes, and who is so near to us that we have no wisdom, no power, no life wholly our own.

–Dresser.

August 25

We are so accustomed to think of the divine nature as wholly unlike and separated from our own character, that it is long ere we can make this realization a power in daily consciousness. We have limited our worship of God to one day in the week, to one place of prayer. We obviously do not know ourselves, do not possess ourselves, and have no permanent centre of repose, until we discover the inward Kingdom of Heaven where God dwells *always*.

—Dresser.

August 26

We must learn that there is something within that will teach a man better than any mere thought of his own,—that he has a wellspring of guidance and inspiration in his own soul. It gives quietness and comfort to know this fact. Nearly everyone has been conscious of such guidance at times. Help also comes to us often during sleep, when the brain is quiet, and the soul watches. God never fails to respond to any call for help and inspiration. All we need to learn is to trust Him.

—Dresser.

August 27

One loses fear,—one ceases to worry about one's friends, or to suffer for wrongs that one is powerless to prevent, when this realization becomes a habit, that God dwells within as well as without. For if God, and not man, is behind events we can safely trust the universe to Him,—and not only the universe, but our friends, our suffering and ignorant fellow-beings—and our own souls. When we genuinely accept this truth we are willing to be led by the Spirit, and we are spared a deal of unnecessary suffering.

—Dresser.

August 28

Education of the *truer* sort brings poise; for it develops individuality; health and strength of intellect, which in turn aids in the attainment of health and strength of body. There is an easiest, simplest way of doing everything, with the least degree of strain and nervous anxiety. "Self-possession forgets all about the body when it is using it." It interposes no obstacle to the physical and mental forces. It discovers the easiest method of concentration through inward repose.

—Dresser.

August 29

One may have a certain bodily poise, yet have no repose of character, and may be the victim of a veritable whirlwind of nervous excitement within. Those who are aware of their own mental development and soul growth are usually conscious of touching a deeper and deeper centre, and with each experience comes added poise and readjustment to life.

—Dresser.

August 30

Every trying experience demands a strengthening of one's faith, a deepening of one's self-possession; for the natural *tendency* is to fear, worry and doubt. We are not sure of ourselves until we have undergone the test of severe experience. Any experience, then, that strengthens this inward repose is rather a blessing than a hardship.

—Dresser.

August 31

Simply to know that every event has an adequate cause, that action and reaction are equal, that experience depends on our attitude of mind, a new directing of the will, and the forces of our being are brought round to correspond. This simple knowledge is enough to give us poise and make us masters.

—Dresser.

September 1

There are as many lines of approach to the "inner centre" as there are temperaments. The great point of starting is this:—Have a method. Have a soul of your own. Be yourself. Think, realize, until you have a measure of un-borrowed conviction, which establishes a centre of repose, and is a source of happiness and contentment, a centre which yields to no outer tumult, but is receptive to the spirit, which never harbors fear or doubt, no matter what the wavering self may say.

—Dresser.

September 2

Never waver. Never forget that the individual belongs to the universal. Never relax hold of that which is deepest, truest, most spiritual in life, come what may, whether it be joy, or sorrow, or illness, or calamity, which life may bring. Find the centre of your being, which rests at last on the love of God. And, when you lose this poise, regain it, as though you would say, "Sit still, my soul: thou at least must not lose thy composure nor thy awareness of the eternal presence of God."

—Dresser.

September 3

Those who are nervously inclined will find it necessary to stop themselves many times a day when they discover that they are under too great pressure. They will find themselves hurrying unnecessarily, or becoming inwardly excited. Oftentimes all that is needed in order to prevent serious mental and physical trouble is to take off this pressure, and find this quiet inward centre where peace reigns. When you have acquired this habit you have taken a great and important step upward.

—Dresser.

September 4

Simply to turn away from self, and all that destroys repose, to the self which knows the supreme peace, is sufficient to give help and strength at any time and in any place. The wise direction of mind opens the door to help. If we *trust,—if we expect it,*–the help will come, whereas the nervous effort to compel it to come will put an obstacle in its pathway.

–Dresser.

September 5

To know how to rest is the great need of our hurrying age. We are over-intense, over-active about things of little account. We have not yet learned the power and supremacy of the spirit, nor the value of quiet, systematic thinking. We struggle after ideas. We read this book and that, and go from place to place in search of the latest and most popular lecturer, instead of pausing to make our own the few great but profoundly simple laws and truths of the spirit. We are unaware of the power of a few moments of silence.

—Dresser.

September 6

It is often in our periods of receptivity that we make our greatest growth. Not while we actively pursue our ideas do we obtain the greatest light. Oftentimes, if the way is dark, and we find no help, it is better to cease striving, and let the thoughts come as they may,—let the power have us; for there is a divine tendency in events, a tendency in our lives which we may fall back upon, which will guide us better than we know, if we listen, laying aside all intensity of thought, and letting the activity settle down to a quieter basis.

—Dresser.

September 7

Part of this teaching can only be verified by experience, and must seem merely theoretical to many readers. But here is a thought that is for every one,—a simple, practical thought that leads to and includes all the rest. Wise silence invites the greatest power in the world, the Supreme Power, the Omnipresent Life. Let us be still in the truest and deepest sense of the word, and feel that Power. It is the Spirit in all things. It surrounds us here and now, in this present life, this beautiful world of nature, this inner world of the soul.

—Dresser.

September 8

This Spirit that is in all things is supreme wisdom and perfect love. It knows no opposition. There is naught to disturb its harmonious, measured and peaceful activity. It is beauty and peace itself. Its love and peace are present here with us. Let us then pause in the midst of our busy lives for a few moments every day—let us enter the silence—let us be still, and peace will enter our hearts. In this restful, happy moment we have won the peace of eternity, and it is ours forever.

—Dresser.

September 9

Who that has communed with the Power of Silence in this way can do justice to the unspeakable joy of that moment of rest and peace? It is not suggestion alone that brings it. It is something more than mere thought. The experience is one of deep inner stillness. The receptivity of the soul invites the Supreme Mind, the Eternal Peace. Hence the soul's attitude is all-important. It must wait with confidence for the inspiration.

–Dresser.

September 10

In entering the Silence, many will find it difficult at first to banish other thoughts; and it is better not to force the stillness to come, but to let the agitation cease by degrees, letting the thoughts come until they quiet down for mere want of conscious attention. When at last the attention no longer wanders, but is poised in the present moment, it is better to cease definite thought altogether. One will then have a sense of incoming Power, and of newness of life, which no other experience can bring.

—Dresser.

September 11

The incoming Power may not be felt at first when the novice enters the Silence, since it is only after repeated trials that one learns *how to become still.* The consciousness will be drawn away from self, and from physical sensation; and this, after all, is the essential,–to rise above self into the nobler world of the Spirit. Some have found it helpful to set aside fifteen minutes each day for quiet receptivity of this deeper sort. Then when trouble or suffering comes, one will not lose one's self-possession, but will know how to obtain strength.

–Dresser.

September 12

Everything in nature seems to have its ebb and flow, its alternation of day and night, of activity and rest, the one blending with the other throughout the seasons and the centuries. There seems to be a corresponding rhythm in human life, with its joys and sorrows, its successes and its ups and downs. In our night of trouble we forget that day will surely dawn again. This soul-experience, this personal evidence that we have been guided, should take all fear from us. The eternal law and fitness of things opens vistas of understanding.

—Dresser.

September 13

If we dwell in eternity, why need we hurry in soul, whatever bodily hurry may be required? Why should we not dwell here in the everlasting present, instead of reaching off somewhere in thought, anticipating the future and death, as though there would ever be a break in the stream of life? If we, as souls, dwell in eternity, is not our life continuous?

—Dresser.

September 14

It is well once in a while to pass in review all that should cause us joy and thankfulness,–to ascend the mountain of thought, whence we may look beyond all the ugly spots in our lives and see their relation,–and, after all, it is a beautiful one–to the great landscape beyond.

–Dresser.

September 15

Our poise is worth little if it fails to give strength and composure in any possible experience. If we habitually realize what it means to dwell in God, what the soul is, and how it is approaching complete realization, and keep the ideal of adjustment to life ever before us, pausing in silent receptivity whenever we become too intense, and becoming powerful and positive through the strength gained, then into the mind will steal a constant renewal of power and illumination, and we will know the real meaning of peace and joy.

—Dresser.

September 16

There is a Tendency which will carry man onward if he will acknowledge it. It will guide him in every detail of life,–it will help him in every moment of trouble. It is with all men–otherwise they could not exist. But to the majority it is unknown, and unrecognized. To turn to it in times of doubt and trouble is to regain one's poise, to become adjusted to life, to gain the truest help. That is what it means to be "led by the spirit."

–Dresser.

September 17

If we follow this "Inner Tendency" rather than the opinions of men, contaminating influences cannot touch us, and fear will have no power over us. Simply to discover that so much depends on our mental attitude is of itself sufficient to work a wonderful change in the lives of those who bear this great truth in mind;—for if we begin life afresh, determined to see the real meaning and spirit of things, old habits of thought, fears and inherited notions will leave us. The road to better health, freedom and happiness is open before us.

—Dresser.

September 18

Happiness, joy, genuine pleasure, and self-denial are expansive emotions, and oftentimes wonderfully catching. With these emotions come self-forgetfulness and lack of constraint. Love is warm,–selfishness is cold and begets self-consciousness and painful awareness of antagonistic sensations. Happiness expands. Fear contracts. We have the power of choice.

–Dresser.

September 19

Be unselfish; have an ideal outlook; see yourself as you would like to be,–healthy,–happy,–well adjusted to life, helpful, wisely sympathetic, and you will have no time to be annoyed, or fearful, or restless, or morbid. This doctrine makes us aware of our own responsibility, and shows us that life is an individual problem. It warns us never to look upon that problem as too difficult to solve, if we approach it hopefully, and full of confidence and good cheer.

–Dresser.

September 20

Is it not our duty to be happy, and forever young in spirit? We have all met people whose very being seems to thrill from some unseen source of happiness. What influence can resist such a power? It is health in the truest sense of the word. It opens one to the renewing, the indwelling energy, by which we exist, whereas *fear* contracts, and causes one to shut out that energy. There is something profoundly unhealthy in our thought if any trouble whatever leads us to suppress this inner joy.

—Dresser.

September 21

Worry and fear play an important part in all varieties of disease, and some people have scarcely a moment's freedom from some tormenting belief or mental picture, want of charity, jealousy, anger, or any emotion which tends to draw one into self, to shut in and contract, is marked in its effect, for if continued, it disturbs the whole organism, and manifests itself as a purely physical disease.

—Dresser.

September 22

Our chief concern is the mode of life that enables one to regain health and to keep it. It is universally admitted that there is a natural healing power resident in the body. This power is common to all, or nearly all, forms of organized life. Many people have learned to relax and to keep quiet like the animals, giving nature a free opportunity to heal their maladies. No one has ever discovered limits to this power. Ultimately speaking it is the power of God, for it is with us every moment of experience.

—Dresser.

September 23

"In physical suffering it is obviously the resident power within that one should think of, and *not the sensation.* Pain rightly understood is beneficent. Through it we are made aware of some injured or diseased part which this resident power has started to heal. If one relaxes the body and mind, nature will respond surely. Whether help is given from the outside, or whatever treatment you pursue, the great aid to healing is in the mental attitude. One either moves with, or hinders the cure."

—Dresser.

September 24

What is God doing with us? What is the ideal towards which the Imminent Life is moving? For everything reveals that the universe is a system, an organism, an adjustment of means to ends for the benefit and development of the whole, inspired by one grand purpose. We did not make the world-order. We cannot change it, and if our life in it is full of misery it is for us to discover *how* we make that misery,– *how* we rebel, *how* we resist,– for it is possible for human beings to vibrate harmoniously *always* with the universal forces. To do so is the real goal.

–Dresser.

September 25

Behind all experience moves one great inspiring Power, developing and perfecting the world. It moves straight towards its goal unceasingly, and without permanent hindrance. Wherein man is adjusted to it, he is already free from suffering. He moves with it, and knows how to become receptive to it. But if he still acts ignorantly he suffers, and is sure to be in conflict until he understands the law of growth.

–Dresser.

September 26

Through our individuality something is bound to come forth, since the resistless power of Almighty God is behind it. Our freedom lies in choosing whether to move with this progressive tendency or against it, for man in his ignorance may oppose and misuse the power that would bless him. He may postpone turning towards the light which some day *must* shine through him, but in so doing he is hugging his sufferings to him, instead of letting go, and learning the meaning of joy.

—Dresser.

September 27

It is a matter of economy to be happy,—to view life and all its conditions from the brightest angle. It enables one to seize life at its best. It calls power to do our bidding. It renews. It awakens. It is a far nobler religion than that creed which causes one to put on a long face, and look serious. There is something wrong in our philosophy if it sanctions melancholy and pessimistic thoughts. A deep and unquenchable spirit of joy is the truest evidence that we believe in the beneficence of the Father.

—Dresser.

September 28

Some people wonder how it is that others who do not seem to be physically strong are able to do so much more in the same length of time. Here is one of the secrets. They have learned how to work. They do one thing at a time, and they do that well, moderately. They live for the time being in and for that particular activity, and there is no wear and tear due to borrowing trouble from other things. But in other words, the attitude of which I speak is optimistic, when one is willing to trust that all will be well.

—Dresser.

September 29

Optimism moves within the harmonious tide of life, and is content to be carried forward. All these states are within our control. All of us may learn to live in the present. If the present is full of hardship, the best way to overcome the hardship is to meet it here and now. Our trials do not seem so hard when we settle down to meet them in their own environment. For the same circumstances which bring the trial also bring the power to meet it.

—Dresser.

September 30

All that we need is here. There is no need to complain of the universe. But we must do our part by learning how to live wisely and profoundly in the eternal present. Life in the present opens the way to the discovery of untold resources in the mental world. There is much wisdom awaiting recognition, and it will be made known to us and through us when we become receptive enough to perceive it. To live in the present is truly to become ourselves, and serve the Higher Power.

—Dresser.

October 1

Not until we begin to live reposefully do we begin to experience the benefits of our powers. Each of us starts with a certain amount of power. That power is sufficient to carry us through life in health, strength and happiness, with abundant liberty to do good, and profit by experience. Right here and now we have sufficient power to live sanely if we would but possess it, acquire poise and use our power wisely. The waste of energy in the average human machine is enormous.

—Dresser.

October 2

We waste energy by the way we walk, by nervous habits of eating, working, and the like. There is an economical rhythmical way to spend our forces which will spare us the nervous wear and tear. It is the little, interior tension and excitement which is the most wearing. One need not become a slow-coach in order to avoid this nervous waste of force. It is possible to move rapidly yet harmoniously and reposefully. Possess yourself *within*. Be at home in your own mental world, and you may move as quickly as you please on the surface.

—Dresser.

October 3

This is a perfectly familiar thought – that the problem of today is sufficient unto today. Yet it is no small attainment to learn how to live in the present. It is a good rule to follow throughout the day, not simply during one's half-hour of silent seclusion. The silent time is needed largely as a preparation for the remainder of the day. Put yourself into the present,– make a fresh start, then make a determined effort to stand by the present. If you catch yourself scattering your forces, living past, present, and future at once, *call yourself back*.

–Dresser.

October 4

If you do not see what is wise for you to do next year, what plans you ought to adopt for the coming month, what you should do tomorrow, ask yourself if there is something for you to do today. The chances are that you will find something that is very well worth doing. Probably you will find more in the living present than you can attend to,–and there you were borrowing trouble for next year! When you have settled upon the wisest thing for today, do it as well as you can,–you will be led to see what to do next.

–Dresser.

October 5

This resource never fails. When in doubt about the future, when in need of guidance, we can at least be true to the best we know *now.* That is all that any one can ask of us. Within the breast there is a guide for all. The wise tendency of the present is related to the wisdom of all time. Brush all else aside, discover the inner sanctuary of your being,—the Holy of Holies, where God speaks to the soul, and the way into the future will open out to you.

—Dresser.

October 6

An anxious mind cannot see clearly for itself or others. How shall we begin the day? First with joyousness, then taking one thing at a time, and doing it well. If plans have been made and cannot be carried out, never mind. If there are interruptions and delays, never mind. Allow no temper or fearing to take possession of you. Find out the good in all experiences.

–K. Newcomb.

October 7

"The world" does not mean this planet or this life. We can live right in the world and not be of it. Jesus said, "I have overcome the world"—while He was yet here. Every one has his own world, for the world is a condition of mind. It is where we believe in material things to the exclusion of spiritual things;—where we feel that we are influenced by our surroundings and people,—where all help must come from without.

—K. Newcomb.

October 8

"The world" means:–Where there is jealousy and therefore strife. Where we are judged, and judge others by externals. Where we fear evil, fear men, fear poverty, conditions, disease, death. "The world" is a fearing condition of mind. How shall we overcome "the world"?–how find Heaven within? We must become conscious of our latent spiritual power. We must kill out all sense of separation from God. It is this sense of separation that keeps us living in "the world."

–K. Newcomb.

October 9

"Be of good cheer." We do not overcome by getting discouraged, for that is a sense of separation from God. When we are strong through consciousness of soul we are of "good cheer." Seeking happiness does not bring it. Success does not come by straining and striving, but by *living.* Keep your ideals high and live up to them, if you would "overcome the world." Get out of "the world" condition of mind by overcoming through control of the personal self by the spiritual self.

–K. Newcomb.

October 10

You will not be a success where you want to be, until you learn to be a success where you are. We attract by our weak points as well as by our strong ones. Learn to lift your mind from your present surroundings if they trouble you. You must do this in order to rise above them or get away from them. While a person or surroundings can disturb you, they have power over you. Become indifferent to them, and the power dies.

—K. Newcomb.

October 11

Indifference to conditions; indifference to the opinions of others; indifference to praise or blame when we have decided which course we will take; this gives poise. When you see a person whose life is harmonious, you may be sure there was a time of struggle before that plane was reached. When there is inharmony, it shows a lack of understanding of law. We can be happy and well, if we choose. No one limits us. No condition limits us. Attitude of mind is the solution.

—K. Newcomb.

October 12

What you get out of a book you carry to it. What you get out of music you carry to it. What you get out of a lecture or a lesson you carry to it. And what is that? Your "capacity to receive." From books, music, lecture, lessons, you get only what you are able to receive. How much you are benefited depends upon your capacity to receive.

–K. Newcomb.

October 13

To be master of a situation does not mean to be limited or repressed. We must bring our tempers, our impatience, our depression, under control. This comes by earnestness, perseverance and courage. There is a calm, not sluggishness nor indolence, which is the result of self-control. You cannot be calm if you worry. You cannot be calm if you doubt. You cannot be calm if you fear. Calmness is like a harmonious musical instrument, a steady vibration. It is a power.

–K. Newcomb.

October 14

It is not circumstances that make us, but we make circumstances. Complaint plants seeds of failure, confidence plants seeds of success. Both will flower and bring forth of their kind. Wavering thoughts, indecision, are dead thoughts, lifeless thinking, and bring weakness into the body. The body reflects mental states. Thoughts of confidence give activity and strength. Egotism is deadness of thought and sometimes results in softening of the brain. A wavering mind is filled with unrest, discontent and doubt.

—K. Newcomb.

October 15

To gain poise we must get peace of mind. Peace of mind comes with feeling perfectly sure that you are in your place and have your work. Being uncertain; believing in chance or fate; wishing we could do something else,—these scatter our forces. Then the power of work does not enter into our development. We work to advantage when we recognize this law and work *with* it.

—K. Newcomb.

October 16

All we learn from others is suggestive, and we profit by it more or less according to our special need. But the question to be answered in our separate minds is, "What does life mean to me?" not, what does it mean to others,—not what do they think it means, but absolutely to myself, what does life mean to me? We suppose that when this question is asked that we have passed beyond the mere external living, that we are seekers after the eternal realities of life.

—K. Newcomb.

October 17

Let us make it one life, and not "this life" and the "next life." What we must desire in life is growth, is knowledge that is to help us not only for time, but for eternity. It is not a simple matter, this question of learning, that will suffice for a day,—but its foundation must be so broad and so sure that it will hold all else that is to come after. Each must have his own method, his own inspiration, but there is this truth that will help us all:—When we are *true* to our highest conception of truth we are true to all who are seeking.

—K. Newcomb.

October 18

In being true, that is, in living in sincerity of purpose, we unfold the spiritual. As this unfolds more and more we get clearer visions of what life means, and have experiences that are most helpful to ourselves. These are interior experiences, experiences where we come into closer communion with our soul, or divine part. The soul like a crystal is clear and perfect—it reflects the divine thought and image.

—K. Newcomb.

October 19

We need decision in regard to overcoming defects in disposition, decision in action, decision in overcoming fear, decision in overcoming impatience, decision in overcoming selfishness, decision in placing the cause of all difficulties in self. Are we living to the best of our knowledge *today*? Poise in our daily living is not an assumed calm. It is an interior stillness where no inharmonies can enter.

—K. Newcomb.

October 20

Every one has had moments of inspiration, but as we develop, inspiration is more frequent. We have an important question to decide. We feel like sinking to our lowest level, but suddenly we are inspired to rise,–to rise above our distress. And as we hold this inspiration, which is a conscious power, we see the horizon clear, and we feel strong to go on. As we become more and more spiritually awakened, our whole life will be an inspiration.

–K. Newcomb.

October 21

We say of some people, "They are such an inspiration." The only way we can help people is to live well ourselves. To trust in "the guidance" to the utmost, never to be discouraged, never faint-hearted, never failing in love, always an inspiration to all who come near us. No gift of knowledge or invention we give the world can equal in inspiration a well-lived life, which is not what we say, but what we are.

–K. Newcomb.

October 22

If we are looking for God in our brother man, instead of being critical and resenting his condition, just to the extent we find God in him, are we an inspiration. He feels that we have found it. He does not know what it is. He does not analyze it. But we have touched the *real* of him, and he is inspired to do his best.

–K. Newcomb.

October 23

A man's world is his present mood. If you are discouraged today your world is hollow. If you have lost by death you are in despair. If you are happy, the world, your world, is a beautiful place. I see the incompleteness of all our lives. We forget that we are surrounded by God's greatness. We forget that we ourselves are capable of greatness. We are troubled in our present mood. We feel limited and unhappy. The smallness of our nature is uppermost.

–K. Newcomb.

October 24

All lives that are controlled by moods are restless. It is the restlessness of people that shows the lack of poise. These look for help. And these are they who, when you present a truth, which if *lived* would make them glad, begin by doubting it before they have even tried to think about it, much less to live it. They are restless and unhappy, and unsettled and yet searching for happiness. Any belief seems better to them than to assume personal responsibility. They want to put the blame on some one, or on some condition.

–K. Newcomb.

October 25

Depression is not a state of trust. You cannot *trust* without joy. Look into your restlessness, find the cause, begin with joy and then trust. You will become conscious of resting in God. As a result the restlessness is going, is fading away. This is not imaginary. You even begin to wonder how you ever could have been restless. Spiritual consciousness *does* satisfy, does *rest*. Help is always at hand when we trust.

–K. Newcomb.

October 26

A prejudice really means prejudging, that is, judging without investigation or understanding of the matter. We claim that things, or ideas concerning things, are so and so, simply because we have a prejudice in our minds against all innovations. Anything out of the old rut annoys or disturbs us, so we run up against the prejudices and call them obstacles. Some people always take the negative attitude of mind. Others always anticipate failure in all undertakings. The depleting effect of them is terrible.

–K. Newcomb.

October 27

Circumstances are always the expression of the individual, and therefore are never an obstacle to that individual. A person suffering from any cause makes the difficulty an obstacle or a stepping-stone. Don't be afraid of anything that presents itself as an obstacle. Meet it with confidence and indifference. You are amply strong enough to meet it and turn it to good account.

—K. Newcomb.

October 28

"All successful men have crossed the Desert of Delay and Disappointment on the way to the Promised Land." One meets with discouraged people. People who have become weary with trying, who feel like giving up the fight. We see this where people work as if they were limited and uncertain in all they do. We even have seen it in those who call themselves Christians. To *encourage* people is our distinct duty. Put new courage into a person, so he will begin again with a fresh impetus.

–K. Newcomb.

October 29

In feeding the mind the important consideration is not cramming the ideas and thoughts of others, but selecting those which will quicken and vitalize. The ideas of others are simply *suggestions* to us, to start into action ideas of our own. Real strength of mind comes from *thinking*,—a little *real* thinking every day. The real thinking rests our minds, just as proper food nourishes our bodies. The idle thinking about "nothing in particular" and the worry and fear thinking, exhaust the mind.

–K. Newcomb.

October 30

People are like children, they want so to be comforted and assured over and over again. If you can teach any one to find his own strength, to find his own poise of mind, you are doing him the greatest kindness possible. It matters not what his occupation may be. The daily duties of every life can test our strength of purpose. We all want the comfort that comes as a result of knowing our strength.

–K. Newcomb.

October 31

Life is continuous,—development is continuous. We do not need rest in a future state any more than we need it now, on our spiritual side. Put yourself in harmony with goodness. We can rest here, and be active here, and enjoy here, and be satisfied here. *Feel* yourself in harmony with the stars, planets, atmosphere, earth and water, with all nature. Find yourself in all these things, and find all these things in yourself. Both are true when we harmonize with the universe.

—K. Newcomb.

November 1

Every day should be a glad beginning. We cannot use the opportunity of yesterday, any more than the mill can use the water that has passed by. But there is new water for today for the mills, and there are new opportunities for each of us today,–all blessed opportunities; not one bad one among them. We will leave out our fears for the future. We will live today without fear. It is joy to live. Anxious people only exist. We will live. Today, this hour, is a privilege.

–K. Newcomb.

November 2

Through faith comes knowledge. It is not enough to have faith alone. Compare the littleness of the personal self, with its pride of opinions, resentfulness, self-pity, and the nobility of the soul, with its greatness, its power. Don't be afraid to make mistakes. Don't be afraid to grow. Knowledge through faith will develop in you quicker than you think, and will lighten all the shadows along the path.

–K. Newcomb.

November 3

People there are who accept the teachings of Jesus Christ to "love thy neighbor as thyself," "to take no thought for tomorrow," "to return evil with good"; yet these same people do not love their neighbor,–they *do* take many anxious thoughts for the morrow, and they do not return evil with good. They separate their lives from their religious belief, they profess faith in God, and live in fear.

–K. Newcomb.

November 4

If we are obedient to our higher selves, we are taught and learn easily. If we are unwilling to learn, if we will not assume the responsibility of our own lives, we are not open to the teaching, and will not learn easily. Experiences are lessons, and come to us in all stages of development. They are our tests of strength and growth. The attitude in which we receive them shows how far along we are in evolution of character.

—K. Newcomb.

November 5

I ask you to have no purpose in your thinking or doing but an aim for right living. A living by high ideals, made practical by having faith in your own spiritual nature; by unfolding it by right thinking and living; by a joyous attitude towards life. Do not let the opinions of people overweigh yours–do not do things and think things just because others do them and think them. Step out of this rank, and become individual, and work out your own thoughts patiently and earnestly.

–K. Newcomb.

November 6

When living from only the intellectual and reasoning side of our nature we have many doubts and fears. When living from our spiritual centre things arrange themselves according to the law of the Spirit. When we make a law of doubt and fear, things also arrange themselves according to *this* law. It is not a question of how you would like things to be, but how you have thought and lived, that will decide the question.

–K. Newcomb.

November 7

A wavering mind is filled with unrest, discontent, and doubt. Tranquillity is the outcome of decision, and we have the power to make our choice. Learn to live in harmony with all conditions and all people. Learn not to resent your surroundings, but live above them. According to the positiveness or the negativeness of your attitude towards life will your surroundings be happy, or colorless.

—K. Newcomb.

November 8

A sense of quiet comes as a result of belief in the higher self. Our work seems easy. We can accomplish so much more than formerly with ease. "He that believeth shall not abide in darkness." Darkness here means ignorance. "Shall not abide in ignorance." First belief, then trust or faith; then we know, or realize, or understand. So we shall not abide in darkness, in ignorance, if we first believe.

–K. Newcomb.

November 9

How shall we become conscious of the Christ within? Everything that is artificial in one's life must be put away. The Christ within is born in simplicity, in seriousness of purpose, in putting self out of mind, in listening, interior hearing, not morbid introspection. It is born in the silence and not in the noise. It brings with it freedom from pinched and cramped conditions, individuality, and confidence in ourselves, power of service, gladness, contentment, joy.

—K. Newcomb.

November 10

When you reach the point where you cannot learn from everybody and everything you are a fossil, whether you are forty, or one hundred and forty. The large mind is the receptive mind. We must have not only circulation of blood, but circulation of thought. We cannot be immovable. "The voice of the Almighty saith, 'Up and onward forevermore.'"

–K. Newcomb.

November 11

Until we are free from all anxiety regarding any matter we are not master of it. A man must educate himself to understand material things, and he must also educate himself to understand spiritual things. No roundness or completeness of character can come from a one-sided development. "All things work out for good with them that trust the Lord"—with this assurance, and the daily proof we have of it, are we not blind and deaf that we do not trust it more?

—K. Newcomb.

November 12

There are too many people who make of life a funeral. What do we gain by being mournful? I can tell you what we get. Disease and inharmony of every kind. Is this gain? When we walk mournfully our bodies are heavy; we drag our feet; our eyes look anxious and sharp. We are weary all the time; all this more or less. How can it be otherwise, since mind affects the body? Joy is a condition of mind–so is sadness. Joy is like oil to machinery. Without it life is friction, and colorless.

–K. Newcomb.

November 13

"Thou shalt be steadfast and thou shalt not fear, because thou shalt forget thy misery, and remember it as waters that pass away." The strong character is the one that stands by its convictions. The first thing to be, is to be steadfast in your desire for truth. We must do away with fickleness and uncertainty. A steadfast nature yields as soon as it is convinced of a truth. An obstinate nature is not steadfast, because it holds on to opinions in defiance of truth, and refuses the revelation.

—K. Newcomb.

November 14

Peace is power. We cannot use our spiritual powers while living in impatience or discontent. Peace is not apathy, it is life itself. We make our mental state an atmosphere which emanates from us, and relates us to all with which we are in harmony. When the mind is poised, body and soul are in health. You can make yourself a target for all unpleasantness if you are mentally wanting in poise. Prove this truth for yourself,—not lightly, but with desire to learn.

—K. Newcomb.

November 15

Poise is harmonious life; it is balance,—the whole man in harmony—physical, intellectual, and spiritual harmony. Before this is acquired we feel helpless, and at the mercy of all that surrounds us. We fear because we have no real sense of power. We are tossed about. But the glory of it all is that each one has within him the power which makes for peace—the divine spark is latent in all. We have only to acknowledge it, and it will lead us aright.

—K. Newcomb.

November 16

Let us rejoice in whatever opportunity comes our way, seeing only good in it, or if we cannot see the good at the present moment, *know it is good without a doubt.* If we make good use of our opportunities, our experiences, we enter into joy. We are not here to have things made easy for us. Neither are we here to have things made hard for us. We make things hard until we learn the truth of how to make our lives harmonious, peaceful, and effective.

–K. Newcomb.

November 17

If discordant thinking is given free course without more or less resistance and repression, control of the actions sooner or later becomes impossible, for such thoughts will ultimately do their work in one way or another. Learning is not necessary to enable a man to stop his discordant thinking and thus save himself from its disastrous consequences–but development of willpower *is* necessary. The simplest and humblest man in all the world can accomplish the acquirement of self-control.

–A. M. Crane.

November 18

Man is meant for happiness, and that happiness is within his reach. "The Kingdom of Heaven is at hand" indeed, and man may dwell therein if he *will*—joy, pleasure, peace, are all the results of right thinking, and there is no reason why every one may not have them. The truth, the beauty, the grandeur, the inspiration, are for every man, and are obtainable by him.

—A. M. Crane.

November 19

Hard work, with a peaceful harmonious mind, never kills any one; and when it is accompanied by sincerity, hope and joy, it builds up the system and prolongs existence instead of shortening it; but worry kills,–and not to stop it is slow but certain suicide, as well as the destruction of much of the joy of one's best and closest friends.

–A. M. Crane.

November 20

Cultivate gladness. Depression disappears just in proportion as one cultivates gladness and serenity. The infinite Father has not given man the aspiration for better things merely to deny him at the last. He does not mock His children. The attainment of this goal is more than a possibility: It is a certainty.

–A. M. Crane.

November 21

We need as much as possible to fasten our thought on life and increasing life,—life greater in its activity than any we have ever yet realized. That is not gained by looking backward. Look forward. Every regret, every mournful thought, takes so much out of your life. It is force used to pile on more misery. It is force used to make the mind color everything with a tinge of sadness. You therefore spread sadness. You have no right to do this.

—Prentice Millford.

November 22

Nothing in Nature, nothing in the universe is at a standstill. Nothing goes backward. A gigantic incomprehensible Force and Wisdom moves all things forward toward greater and higher powers and possibilities. You are included in and are part of this Force. You as a spirit are made in God's image. God is eternal life, eternal joy—eternal serenity. The more of these characteristics you reflect, the nearer you are to the infinite Spirit of Good.

—Prentice Mulford.

November 23

To get enjoyment from everything is to get life from everything. To get life from everything is to develop power, and a capacity to live *truly*. "Ennui" is sickness. When we don't know what to do with ourselves,–when everything seems "flat, stale, and unprofitable," we have temporarily lost our hold of the great Fountain of Life, the Supreme Mind and Power.

–Prentice Mulford.

November 24

A thought attracts thought of like kind. Keep any thought fixed in your mind, say the thought of strength or health, and you attract to you more and more of the thought-element of strength and health. Keep in mind the idea of force, "go-ahead," push, and you at tract to you the element which gives you force, push and "go-ahead." For thought is an invisible substance, as real as air, water, or metal. It acts apart from your body,—it goes from you to others, far and near; it attracts to you the people and things you need.

—Prentice Mulford.

November 25

Every thought of yours has a literal value to you in every possible way. The strength of your body, the strength of your mind, your success in business, and the pleasure you give out to others, depends on the nature of your thoughts. If your thought is despondent, jealous, carping, *it repels*. If cheerful, hopeful, and full of earnest desire to do the most good possible to any one you meet, though but for a single minute, *it attracts*. This is an absolute law. Joyous thoughts spread joy, and bring back joy, and so it is with everything.

–Prentice Mulford.

November 26

Your value and charm for others, as a companion, depends far more on what you think than on what you say. If your thought is all pure, clean, bright, confident, and courageous, you are a value. and an increasing value, wherever you go. People will always be glad to see you. You bring to them a power and strength. Your thought helps to strengthen their bodies. Thy feel better for seeing you. You are a fountain of health and pleasure wherever you go.

—Prentice Mulford.

November 27

Mind is "magnetic," because it attracts to itself whatever bears relation to the thought it fixes itself upon, or whatever it opens itself to. Allow yourself to fear, and you will fear more and more. Cease to resist the tendency to worry, and you open the door to it, and invite it in, and all the currents of worry emanating from millions of worrying people will be attracted to you, and you will be carrying a load of worry which will eventually materialize into bodily sickness. Set your mind on health and courage and the like currents will be drawn to you.

—Prentice Mulford.

November 28

Every success in any grade of life has been accomplished through spiritual power, through unseen force flowing from one mind, and working on other minds far and near. This force is as real as the force in your arm, which you apply when you lift a stone. Persistent resolve on any purpose, is a real and attracting force or element, drawing constantly more and more aids for carrying out that resolve. Every second of wise demand brings an increase of power. Such increase is never lost to us, once we have ma de it ours.

–Prentice Mulford.

November 29

When you realize the injury done you through any kind of troubled thought, you will then commence to acquire the power of throwing off such thought. Christ said:–"Resist the devil, and he will flee from you." An ugly or melancholy mood of mind is a devil. It can make us sick, lose us friends, and lose us money. When in mind you commence to resist any kind of injurious thought, you are constantly gaining more and more power for resistance.

–Prentice Mulford.

November 30

When men and women believe in themselves, and have learned to trust to their own power to do anything which is worthy of their higher nature, and while accepting helps from others, regard always the helps as secondary to their own power for pushing things ahead, it means they have learned that they are really parts of the Infinite arts, they have Power, and that, as more or less of the qualities of that Power for doing, for accomplishing anything they may set about.

–Prentice Mulford.

December 1

Faith is spiritual knowledge. It is entirely different from the knowledge gained from books, or from any ordinary process of education. It is that knowledge which the spirit gains as it goes out and lives in the invisible world to which it belongs. It is not merely knowledge. It is an acting and immediate power for moving events and persons. The spiritual realm of life is infinitely larger than seen and felt by the physical senses. We live and move in it, unconscious of its existence. Only the divine in us is conscious of it.

—Prentice Mulford.

December 2

Faith is a wisdom and a force in nature far above that based on human reason. It is a force which may come to us to do things seemingly inconsistent and imprudent, yet when in the course of years the whole is summed up, we find that we have been led to better results than could otherwise have been gained. In such cases we have been "led by the Spirit," or in other words, obeyed the promptings of the spiritual senses, instead of following that rule of life governed entirely by the physical senses.

—Prentice Mulford.

December 3

In saying that your faith can be continually increased by prayer, we mean that by constant prayer to the Supreme Power, you will continually receive clearer and more powerful thought; that your spiritual and more powerful senses will come more and more into practical use; that you will rely and depend on them more and more and receive clearer and deeper insight as you grow in the consciousness of them. The mental attitude of prayer will become habitual whether you are conscious of it or not.

–Prentice Mulford.

December 4

When you cannot decide what is best to do in any matter whatsoever, rest your mind, and wait for the prompting of the Supreme Spirit. It will come to you in the shape of an idea, an inspiration, an event, an opportunity. You have not stopped while you so waited. You have all that time been carried to the idea, the inspiration, the event, the opportunity, and it also has been carried or attracted to you.

—Prentice Mulford.

December 5

It is worth repeating over and over again that your health, your fortunes, your success in any undertaking depends entirely on your predominant mental condition, or frame of mind. If that frame of mind is buoyant, hopeful, courageous, always looking on the bright side and towards success, never desponding, or if so inclined, fighting off despondency, then you are certain of ultimate success, for then you are sending out the force which attracts success.

–Prentice Mulford.

December 6

The more you cultivate and live in the consciousness of the power of thought, the stronger will your faith becomes in these silent forces, which will bring you health, peace, happiness and success,—for as this silent power in you increases, as increase it must if held to, you will receive more and more proofs, and ever stronger proofs of what it can do for you. For when you hold persistently to the successful mental state, you become a magnet, ever drawing people to aid you, as you in return can aid them.

—Prentice Mulford.

December 7

Having a defined purpose in view, the atmosphere of thought you carry with you in your dealings with others, is a power stronger to aid you than your spoken words. Because all who come in contact with you will feel this atmosphere. If you have confidence in your ability, if you are honest to the core, they will *feel* that confidence and honesty after you leave them, and as you persist in your purpose, they will feel it more and more, for that power is always acting upon them.

–Prentice Mulford.

December 8

There is a class of people who, when in difficulties any one suggests a way out, instantly raise objections, and find difficulties in the plan proposed. When in thought we so find difficulties, we actually make them. To lay awake nights and brood, devise, turn over or invent possible coming troubles, is force and industry ill employed in preparing the way for those troubles.

—Prentice Mulford.

December 9

In all undertakings we must press on in mind to the successful result. We must see in mind the thing completed, the undertaking advancing and ever growing stronger. To spend time and force in looking back and living past troubles or obstacles over again, and out of such living and mental action to conjure more difficulties or oppositions, is literally to spend time and force in destroying your undertaking, or in manufacturing obstacles to put in your own way.

—Prentice Mulford.

December 10

Life is a continual advance forward. If we are advancing forward, it is better to look forward. And all are advancing, even the dullest, and grossest, the most perverse. A mighty, eternal and incomprehensible force pushes us all forward. But while all are being so pushed, many linger and look back. Unconsciously they oppose this force. To do so is to court evil, pain, disease, and distress.

—Prentice Mulford.

December 11

Whatever the mind is set upon, or whatever it keeps most in view, that it is bringing to it, and the continual thought must at last take form and shape in the world of seen and tangible things. This fact is the corner-stone of your happiness or misery, permanent health and prosperity, or poverty. Our thought is the unseen magnet ever attracting its correspondence in things seen and tangible. As we realize this more and more clearly, we shall be more careful to think happiness and success, instead of misery and failure.

—Prentice Mulford.

December 12

Life is fuller of possibilities of happiness than have ever been realized. The real life means a perpetual and ever-increasing maturity. It means an ever-increasing freshness—a perception and realization of all that is grand, wonderful and beautiful in the universe. Life is eternal in the discovery and realization of these joys. Their source is inexhaustible. Even in so-called ordinary things we do not get out of our lives but a fragment of the pleasure they are capable of giving us.

—Prentice Mulford.

December 13

The only persons who can talk *safely* with each other, and serve as mutual confessors each to the other, must be on the same plane, and in the same current of thought. They must see things with the same eye. They must understand each other. They must divine and interpret each other's motives and character through that intuition, or unspoken commun-ion which always exists between kindred minds, and by which a few words tell more than can be explained in an hour of spoken conversation.

—Prentice Mulford.

December 14

The body is literally banged to pieces by the mental action and mood of unrest. Thoughts flying to no purpose without control here, there, and everywhere, and on everything, hour after hour, and day after day, do literally tear the physical machine to pieces. Sleeplessness comes from lack of mental control or the habit of never-ceasing, spasmodic, fitful thought, leading surely to spasmodic, fitful, physical acts, and if the mind cannot control the body in the daytime, neither can it control it at night.

—Prentice Mulford.

December 15

Keep away as much as you can from despondent, reckless, and purposeless people. If of necessity you are thrown in their company, make up your mind that you will not absorb any of their thought. Then you put on a positive protective armor against such absorption. Those who walk together in one mind or belief are of great help to each other, but those who try to walk together with differing minds or beliefs, only cripple each other. Mutual belief generates force in both.

–Prentice Mulford.

December 16

You carry into company not only your body, but what is of far more importance, your thought, or mood of mind, and this thought or mood, though you say little or nothing, will create with others an impression for or against you, and as it acts on other minds will bring you results favorable or unfavorable according to its character. What you think is of far more importance than what you say or do, because your thought never ceases for a moment its action upon others.

—Prentice Mulford.

December 17

Can we not always tell when a person has found his spiritual centre? There is a tranquillity, a repose, a breeziness about him. You feel that the air he breathes is more invigorating than the atmosphere in which most people live. There is a certain unlimited air about him,–an air of the open plains or mountain tops, an exhilaration which lifts you up and out of all your difficulties, and makes you know that you yourself are superior to and master of all conditions that heretofore seemed to master you.

–K. Newcomb.

December 18

"The Deity" will "shine through" each one of us, if we will let It have Its way. Do not be afraid to trust that higher nature which is leading you on. We cannot trust too much. We gain absolutely nothing until we do trust. It is pathetic, in a way, to see people who are really afraid to let go of the old self and trust the inner leading of the soul. They still cling to the intellect and externals, fearing the intuition and the inner life, as if a devil lurked there to destroy us, instead of our Creator. Faith develops. Doubt kills.

–K. Newcomb.

December 19

Help is near. Peace is close to us. Happiness is at our door. It comes to us in proportion to our receptivity to it, our faith in it. We are equal to any task, any emergency, any struggle, for God is here. We need not go anywhere to find Him. He is omnipresent. Life is a constant readjustment. It requires a daily renewal of one's faith. But it is priceless knowledge to know that we are equal to any occasion if we let the divine that is in us lead the way.

—Dresser.

December 20

We need to guard ourselves even in loving ministry against the sacrifice of individuality. It is indispensable to a true life to think from its own centres. It is not always wise to force ourselves to look at matters from the stand-point of another. Much yielding against our judgment is a weakness. To give in just for the sake of peace shows indolence of character. As one develops individuality he is very sure to be misunderstood by his domestic circle.

–Newcomb.

December 21

We too often hasten through the passing days with but scanty enjoyment or stolid endurance, looking hazily to some distant time for the fulfilment of desire. The best conditions for future happiness lie in the largest possible appreciation of the present. This is a truth we all admit; yet we spend our lives in following happiness as a phantom, and blinding ourselves to present good. There are wells of water in the dreariest desert; yet many travelers have perished chasing a mirage

—Newcomb.

December 22

Enter any graveyard and read the records carved upon the stones. Here we find many men and women who killed themselves with worry, fretted themselves to death by their antagonism to the conditions in which they lived, and for which they found no remedy. They were slain by the fears which they had nursed in their own breasts. The doctors called their trouble "nervous prostration" or "pneumonia." Here are others that poisoned themselves by temper, etc. Egotism is written over most of the graves.

–Newcomb.

December 23

All spiritual progress and enfoldment which is the result of individual aspiration never has to be done over, because it has been accomplished not *for* one, but *by* and *in* him. It is walking upon one's own feet without external aid. It is drawing directly from the Infinite Fountain of life, love, and good, through the channel of one's own being. It develops self-reliance and spiritual independence, and strengthens those inner ties which bind every human soul to the parent "Oversoul."

–H. Wood.

December 24

Let no one mistake for sensitiveness that which is born of selfishness, jealousy, envy or egotism, for they have no connection whatever. The person who is always getting "hurt" by some fancied slight, some lack of appreciation or attention, should never hide behind the plea of being sensitive, but should face the truth squarely, and recognize that jealousy and self-love—not self-respect—breed the thoughts which wreck his happiness.

—Crane.

December 25

It should be distinctly noted that the suffering commonly attributed to sensitiveness does not come from that source, but comes solely from the discordant thinking which, through lack of mental control, is allowed to follow. Because of this entire separateness between sensitiveness and thinking, and because the suffering comes from discordant thinking and not from sensitiveness, the most keenly sensitive person may so train himself that he can stop his discordant thinking and thus avoid all injurious consequences.

—Crane.

December 26

Humanity depends upon sympathy for more than it realizes, and constantly receives it in unnoted ways. We do not understand why, but a sense of peace and strength comes as we look into some face seen perhaps for the first time; we hear a voice, and something within us responds in harmony. No one can measure its influence when this sympathy goes out from one whose soul is so filled with love for all humanity that he has an ear for every heart-pulse that is beating. Such a one gives out sympathy in joy and sorrow, without thought of self.

—Crane.

December 27

It has been said that "next to love, sympathy is the divinest passion of the human heart." It might well be said that true sympathy is born of that love which Jesus, the Christ, bade us have for one another – a love which helps always, which is pure in thought, and word, and deed; which seeks always to elevate and strengthen. Of such loving sympathy there can never be too much. It may be given full range, for its fruit is always harmony. It has helped thousands back to life, health, and happiness; while its opposite, born of apprehension and fear, has proved fatal to many other thousands.

–Crane.

December 28

Some people show their discordant thoughts when they visit a sick friend. They commiserate them,—tell them how badly they look, sympathize with them with the sympathy which destroys, and enlarge upon the more serious phases of their disease. These people seem happy when they can tell one who is ill about the extreme suffering of others in a like condition; and if they know of some one who has died of a similar disease, they retail all the particulars to the sufferer who lies there at their mercy. They think themselves comforters. *They are human vampires.*

—Crane.

December 29

The woman who said she "spent half her time doing things, and the other half worrying because she had done them," belongs to a very numerous and uncomfortable family. To worry over or regret what is past and gone is time worse than wasted, for it *does not change anything,* and no activity drains the life energies as this mental torture does. It robs one of sleep, sours the disposition, warps the judgment, and makes the mind weak and vacillating. This is true of every form of worry or anxiety. It can destroy both mind and body.

—Crane.

December 30

One individual with the worry habit can poison the atmosphere for all with whom he is associated, for mental discord is easily communicated, and others are made more or less miserable, either by discordant sympathy, or condemnation. Anxiety and worry about the future have their beginning in uncertainty and doubt, and these soon develop into expectancy of evil things that in all probability would never happen. This vice, for it is a vice, becomes persistent and positive, unless a mental control is established quickly.

—Crane.

December 31

If we desire habitually to scatter sunshine and health among our fellows, wherever we meet them, not only our deeds and words, but our facial expressions and our thoughts themselves, must be well controlled and cheerful. If the right mental habits are established, all the external expressions will take care of themselves without attention or effort, and our presence alone will carry suggestions of gladness wherever we go.

–Crane.